FAITH FOR
TOMORROW

FAITH FOR
TOMORROW

DANIEL O. DUGAN

PFLAUM PRESS   DAYTON, OHIO

230
587 f
7233 8
Dec., 1970

Library of Congress Catalog Card Number: 72-93004

Pflaum Press
38 West Fifth Street
Dayton, Ohio 45402

To Judith Jean

CONTENTS

PREFACE

I have written this book as a member of the Christian community, addressing it primarily to other members of that community. It is intended for Christians who find themselves thinking about the concept of faith and its implications, and who choose to read these reflections on the subject.

The book is concerned with Christian faith, its nature and its claims. Faith usually takes social and institutional forms: Christians are members of churches and congregations. Although I have not discussed Catholicism at length, in those sections in which I do make reference to it, there is some value for Christians of other denominations who face similar questions concerning their own institutional forms.

So many theological works are inaccessible to college students and educated American Christians in general because of the specificity of the subject matter and the technicality of their styles. Without attempting to be "popular" in the pejorative sense of the word, I have attempted to speak clearly and relatively nontechnically, mainly because of the audience intended, most of whom are not theologians. For those readers who might appreciate my suggestions for further readings in the particular topics to which I have referred, I have included short bibliographies for consultation.

I present this book without presumption. It is largely the result of the many kind reactions expressed to my short articles in *America* and *The Catholic World,* reactions which invariably included suggestions that I give fuller treatment to the themes dealt with in those articles. I am grateful to those who expressed those reactions.

I am aware of the tendency in some books to create caricatures of non-Christian "challenges" to religious faith in order to proceed to demolish them, thus vindicating the right of Christians to remain securely unreflective in their faith, confident that they still possess the truth. Though I have included references to some serious questions posed by non-Christians concerning faith, I have also included in the lists of suggested readings some titles which represent the views of those to whose positions I have referred.

I am grateful to Miss Kim Higgins for her assistance in preparing this material. I am indebted to Miss Molly Dugan for her hours before the typewriter. And I thank Prof. Peter D. O'Neill for his encouragement and for his careful criticisms.

1:PROBLEMS OF FAITH (I)

1. NONRELIGIOUS REVIVAL

Histories of Christian doctrine describe an era in the religious history of the West which may have ended in our own day. Vatican II, some say, was the council which ended it all. Because that council was the first major or ecumenical council in the history of Christianity at which bishops did not convene for the purpose of defining Christian doctrine against the challenges of heretical aberrations, they say, it is unique. Because no doctrinal pronouncements emerged from the council, solemn and binding seriously upon the faith of all Christians, optimists announce the end of the era of dogma, of defining or setting limits to Christian belief in a defensive manner.

Cardinal Leon-Joseph Suenens, for example, claims that the renewed Church of the 1960's has become a Church of dialogue, one which has shed its defensiveness and hesitancy to encounter the real problems of men, and which is witnessing to the presence of hope in the modern world.[1]

There are others, however, who interpret the situation more pessimistically. They would admit that there was something exciting about the old days of the heretic hunts. There were times when the streets of Alexandria were red with the blood of antagonists in doctrinal disputes. Roman emperors and European prelates, as well as most of the populations in their lands, have throughout the history of Christendom reacted with concern to threats of heresy. Nearly everyone was a Christian and was in-

[1] Cardinal Leon-Joseph Suenens, *Coresponsibility in the Church* (New York: Herder and Herder, 1968).

1

terested in religious affairs. Reflective persons were sometimes elated, sometimes distraught, but always interested in theological developments. The religious atmosphere was perpetually charged.

However, it has become obvious today that the departure of the continued presence of heretical threats in the Church is a sign of a more important and widespread element in the West: a seeming lack of interest in religion and theology. The only persons who appear to be much interested in such matters are clerics and theologians—and scientists and philosophers—in the process of explaining the world of man without relying on the hypothesis of God.

Thus, say those more pessimistic, the religious atmosphere has become decreasingly charged. The heretics have virtually all disappeared, because there simply is not the general interest in theology anymore. Perhaps Vatican II was significant, therefore, because it was in effect the first admission by the oldest Christian Church of all that it is indeed irrelevant, intellectually and sociologically, to the rest of the world. The key word at the council, "aggiornamento," calls for *change*. Vatican II, therefore, instead of being the beginning of a new and hopeful epoch, may perhaps signal the beginning of the end of the Christian religion in its present forms. This is a possible interpretation.

It is too early to tell which interpretation is correct. Death-knells of Christianity have sounded before. A phenomenon which bears on the question is a kind of religious revival which is occurring in the West, partly outside the boundaries of institutional Christian denominations and churches. Dr. Harvey Cox has pointed to this phenomenon in connection with the "hippie movement." [2] According to Dr. Cox, the motivation underlying the movement in its purest forms is clearly religious.

The revival, however, is equally noticeable among the "straight" students in the classrooms of quiet universities throughout the

[2] Harvey Cox, "God and the Hippies," *Playboy* (Dec., 1967).

country, including state colleges and universities. Scholars of religion and philosophy, such as Prof. Alan Watts, speak regularly to large university audiences concerning the beliefs of Hindus and Buddhists. Courses in Eastern religions attract throngs of students at universities everywhere. Some institutions are creating departments of religious studies in response to the growing demand by the students.

The phenomenon is the emergence of the quest for religious truth and meaning, especially among young people. The Beatles and Mia Farrow have pursued the Maharishi Mahesh to India in search of spiritual fulfillment. Many other young people are searching, outside the boundaries of institutional Western Christian churches, looking toward the religious visions of the East. Though religion has not always attracted youth, it seems that today it is their judgment that the religious question is ultimate, and that their own Christian traditions cannot answer that question. Why? Their own traditions mirror in too many ways the economic scale of values informing the society out of which they have "dropped."

Scientific humanism was the "sophisticated" position of the young intellectuals for a time. Prescinding from the debate about religion, this position advocates a commitment to humanity, an involvement in programs of social amelioration. The question of God's existence has been decided in the negative, on the basis of scientific advances. But this has proved to be inadequate. Largely uninterested in the debate about the existence or non-existence of a God, many young people simply presuppose that man himself poses a problem which is not completely soluble on the humanistic level. They do not feel a compulsion to prove the existence of God; they desire to locate and make contact with the "ground of their being," which they identify as love.

The religious atmosphere in the West may be changing once more because of these young people, who may be introducing a phase in religious history in which men shall reject as irrelevant not only present forms of religious answers, but also the religious questions of today.

2. RELIGIOUS REVIVAL

The prefiguration of this new religious phase is also occurring within institutional religious boundaries. The underground church movement in the United States is a sign that Christians are finding new and more vital forms of Christian worship. The movement itself, although it sometimes creates small groups of initiates whose principal concern lies in the development of their own intramural person-to-person relationships, will perhaps give way to the implementation of formally Christian programs of social effectiveness. The fact remains, however, that this kind of interest exists in this country as a relatively new phenomenon.

Readers who frequent Christian bookstores have noticed an increased rate in the publication of religious and theological materials. Catholic universities such as Marquette, Fordham, St. Louis, Notre Dame and Manhattanville have initiated and developed graduate programs in theology and religious education, discovering that annual applications far exceed the numbers of students who can be accommodated. Harvey Cox, James Pike, Charles Davis and James Kavanaugh are some of the many authors whose books concerning religious matters have enjoyed widespread popularity. The major weekly newsmagazines, such as *Time* and *Newsweek*, find ample material to be able to provide regularly interesting and informative columns concerning religious developments. The religious atmosphere within the churches and the country as such during the past twenty years has intensified.

But many Christians cannot share in the benefits which such a revival should provide for them. At the same time that Christians are demonstrating a real thirst for theological treatments germane to their lives, many of them are frustrated. One reason is that, while there is no shortage of books being published, many of them reflect a concern for relatively restricted areas of interest. For example, during the past few years in Catholic theology, books dealing with the documents of Vatican II, attempting to explain, modify and accelerate the process of Catholic renewal, have been numerous. Books such as these, while they are concerned with important and interesting matters, for example, the relationship between freedom and authority within the Church, episcopal collegiality and liturgical renewal, leave some readers unsatisfied or frustrated because they do not concern themselves with more basic religious issues.

By "more basic religious issues" I mean such matters as faith and Revelation, their natures and functions in the lives of Christians. If the author of a book dealing with liturgical renewal, for example, develops the theme that sacraments are professions of Christian faith, he sometimes necessarily presupposes that "faith" means something specific to his readers. He sometimes presupposes that Christians are one in what they believe, and that they have managed to integrate what they believe with the way in which they live. But this is not so. Even though all Christians *should* understand what they mean when they use the word "faith," many do not. Authors must be highly selective in their choice of subject matter lest every treatment becomes a kind of vast compendium of theology. But authors urging the progress of ecclesial renewal would be even more effective in bringing it about if they could build upon the presupposition that all Christians understand the meaning of the term "faith."

I do not mean to suggest a "back to the catechism" movement. The word "catechism" signifies an approach to religious faith which, although it confronts basic issues, is too narrowly conceived. Pat questions and answers are inadequate to the task of understanding faith. Such an approach was born in a time when the old apologetic was the style. At that time a Christian learned the various elements of his faith by rote, partly in order to be able to defend his faith against the challenges of unbelievers, and possibly even to convert them in the process. Conversion might occur if the believer succeeded in demonstrating the reasonableness of his faith, by proving the existence of God and the immortality of the soul to the heathen.

The approach of the old apologetic is no longer predominant. But there has emerged no new apologetic to replace it. Though faith does not live on the pages of catechisms, it is disastrous to react against the old apologetic by abandoning the entire attempt to demonstrate faith's reasonableness. A new apologetic is necessary, not to "prove" Christianity's truth to unbelievers, but to meet the serious demand by Christians themselves for rational scrutiny of their basic beliefs. What is faith? How is it pertinent to the most important questions of modern human life? Discussions of secondary or ecclesiastical issues will be more effective when the central teachings of Christianity are intelligible to Christians themselves.

There are too many Christians in the Catholic tradition, for example, who can involve themselves in parish liturgical renewal because they instinctively recognize the value of Masses in which people are active participants instead of passive spectators. Their evaluation of a more dynamic liturgy is positive, and they are thankful that they are not subjected to the anachronistic forms of the Mass according to which their friends in other dioceses attempt to worship. Many people are involved in liturgical renewal because they feel that it must take place. They feel this way, not because their understanding of their faith leads naturally to a desire for liturgical renewal, but despite an understanding of faith which is very narrowly conceived.

There have been excellent books and articles during the past few years concerning faith and Revelation. Bernard Lonergan, Karl Rahner and Otto Muck are among contemporary Catholic Christian theologians and philosophers who have worked creatively and effectively to examine the possibilities of faith, its kinds and degrees of certainty and its relationships with other conscious activities in man.[3] Their method, the transcendental method, has been very effective in this regard, partly because it brings to the metaphysical discussion of the concept of faith the benefits of Western philosophy since the time of Immanuel Kant. This method provides a way for the philosopher to understand the foundations for the activity of faith through an analysis of the operations of consciousness and awareness in the knowing human being, thus basing the claim of faith to knowledge in human noetic experience.

But the transcendental method is inaccessible to most Christians, for it presupposes an extensive background and participation in Western philosophy as well as the free time and energy required to develop philosophical understanding. Most people have neither. They are neither philosophers nor theologians, and have no desire to be. Most Christians are not members of the academic community in which the most fruitful theological studies of faith occur. But this does not mean that most Christians, as members of the people of God, do not have the right to the benefits of theological advancement.

There have been recently a number of works on the concept of Revelation which have been well received and widely read. Their authors include Avery Dulles, Gabriel Moran and Rene Latourelle.[4] The work of these theologians, especially of Brother Moran, has been effective in speaking intelligibly to members of the Christian community outside the academic sphere. In re-

[3] Karl Rahner, *Spirit in the World*, trans. William Dych (New York: Herder and Herder, 1968); Otto Muck, *Transcendental Method*, trans. W. Seidensticker (New York: Herder and Herder, 1968); Bernard Lonergan, *Insight* (New York: Philosophical Library, 1965).

[4] Gabriel Moran, *Catechesis of Revelation* (New York: Herder and Herder, 1966); *Scripture and Tradition* (New York: Herder and Herder, 1963); *Theology of Revelation* (New York: Herder and Herder, 1966). Avery Dulles, *Theology of Revelation* (Washington, D.C.: Corpus, 1968); Rene Latourelle, *Theology of Revelation* (Staten Island, N.Y.: Alba House, 1967).

jecting "essentialist-propositional" theories of Revelation, these scholars have incorporated personalistic categories into their analyses, as well as a more realistic sense of historicity.

By "essentialist-propositional" theories of Revelation, I mean the tendency to *define* Revelation as a "something" rather than to describe it as a process. For example, the "truths of Revelation are as follows. . . ." The presupposition is that Christian Revelation can be dissected, expressed completely in propositions and specific teachings.

An approach, on the other hand, is personalistic if it treats Revelation not as a series of propositional truths, but as a "dialogue" between God and man by which God reveals himself (not teachings about himself) to human persons. Because human persons are temporal creatures, such an approach acknowledges the growth of the relationship between God and man in history.

It is regrettable that, despite the presence of many books reflecting this new approach, many Christians have not assimilated it. This is partly because the language of personalism is unfamiliar to them.

At least part of the problem concerns the terminology of the newer theological approaches, as illustrated by experiences of university theology instructors. Many an instructor has, in the courses he teaches, had to "demythologize" his presentation, to rid himself of terminology which, though English, arises from a background and intellectual history foreign to the minds of his students.

There is another difficulty which arises. In courses in Christology and World Religions, while attempting to present Christian teachings intelligibly, instructors often confront such questions as, "What does it mean to say that Christ is God?" "Is Christ necessary to Christianity?" "What relevance does a belief in the divinity of Christ have for our lives?" Why are these questions significant? "Proofs" of the divinity of Christ have been labeled "old apologetics" in Catholic theology for some years now. But it seems that students have not kept themselves abreast of the trends. For they are interested not only in how well Christian teachings can be expressed, but also in why those teachings make sense. Theologians may presuppose the answers to these questions in fraternal discussions, and concentrate on subtler points. But in the classrooms they often find that their students do not share those presuppositions.

How is it possible to meet the questions of university students, whose education in grammar and high schools has led them to consider the gift of faith to be a treasure to be guarded, protected against the attacks of the city of man? How urge them, on the basis of their faith, to work creatively to implement the Christian vision in the world if they have been conditioned not to demand that faith be integrated with human life as such?

Liturgical renewal is an interesting process in this country, claiming the time and energies of many thousands of bishops, priests, laymen and laywomen. But its ultimate success will demand that those persons have faced their own faith honestly and deeply, and have formed an understanding of their faith which they can integrate with their daily lives.

Similar observations could be made concerning educated adult Christians, many of whom have never really allowed themselves to question their faith. Rather, they compartmentalize it, protect it—and isolate it. An important study, that of the clinical psychologist Dr. John Hinton, is an examination of, and report upon, the behavior of dying persons. It indicates that some people who refer to themselves as religious persons throughout their lives are as starkly terrified of death as nonreligious individuals.[5] Their understanding of their faith or religion has never penetrated deeply enough into their psyches. Indeed, often there has been no understanding. There has been only blind acceptance of religious propositions. Never having integrated religion with their normal human experiences, they cannot integrate their

[5] John Hinton, *Dying* (Baltimore: Penguin Books, 1967).

faith with death as they confront it. One reason for the lack of integration is that they have never approached their faith with real honesty and openness, seriously attempting to determine its inherent adequacy to their experience.

There is a great need for a new apologetic. It may be beneficial to reject the previous overemphasis on the reasonableness of Christian faith, because of the "catechism" form which that emphasis assumed, and because its purpose was partially to convince and convert unbelievers to Christianity. Because Revelation was presented as a series of propositional truths, demonstrations could be attempted. But to discard such an approach is not to erase the necessity for reasonable examination by *Christians* of their Revelation and their faith.

Christians must understand how their faith adequately accounts for human experience as they live it, and for their world as they live in it. Studies of the reasonableness of Christian faith are necessary, not for the sake of "proving the faith" to heathens, but for the sake of integrating faith with the daily lives of Christians.

The language of the new apologetic, furthermore, must not be highly technical or exclusive. It must not even be "religious," in the pejorative sense of the word: as pertaining to specifically denominational concerns and values. Dietrich Bonhoeffer, in his *Letters and Papers from Prison*, called for the nonreligious interpretation of biblical categories.[6] By that he meant, essentially, that Christians should stop talking so much about God, and should begin acting like Christ, the man for others. According to Bonhoeffer, the churches must cease their "spiritually incestuous" programs of self-justification, committing themselves rather to programs of social action. It is possible and necessary to show how and why Christians must think and talk about their faith and its claims to truth, while benefiting from Bonhoeffer's critique and suggestions.

---

[6] Cf. Dietrich Bonhoeffer, *Letters and Papers from Prison* (New York: Macmillan, 1967), pp. 160–70.

It is necessary that Christians think and speak of what they believe. As Father Bernard Cooke has pointed out, Christian social involvement necessarily proceeds from Christian understanding.[7] A new apologetic would integrate that understanding with human experience in this world. But it still acknowledges the necessity for *understanding*. Many Christians are frustrated by their inability to integrate the "truths" of faith with their lives. Christians must see if, why, and how their professions of faith commit them to worldly involvement. Confronting the basic issues of faith and Revelation precedes and underlies all other speculations and interests.

What follows immediately is an attempt to indicate more clearly some of the ways in which Christians come to acknowledge their frustrating inability to relate what they believe to how they live. It is an attempt to speak to the frustration of the Christian whose faith is seeking understanding. Why does religious faith remain so isolated in the lives of persons? One answer to that question is historical: because of the manner in which it has been defined. What have been the practical consequences of the way in which it has been defined?

Unintended is any proof of the reasonableness of Christianity to unbelievers, although certain implications for that ongoing dialogue will be present. I speak to a contemporary experience within the Christian tradition: the frustration at being unable to find works dealing with the basic issues of faith and Revelation in nontechnical language.

3. MANY INDICATIONS OF ONE PROBLEM

As we have seen, there is an important distinction between Christians attempting to speak reasonably about their faith to non-Christians, and attempting to articulate aspects of their faith intelligently to themselves as the basis for understanding the re-

[7] Bernard Cooke, *Christian Involvement* (Chicago: Argus Communications Co., 1966).

lationship of that faith to their concrete situations of life. We have designated the former enterprise as the "old apologetic" and the latter necessity as the "new apologetic." Implied, of course, is confronting the question, "What does the label 'Christian' mean?" How does Christian faith relate to everyday life? It is this problem, the value of Christian faith in the lives of Christians, which calls for a new apologetic, and which occupies our interest.

The problems which contribute to the frustrating inability of Christians to integrate their faith with their own lives arise often as a result of confrontations with unbelievers. The problem arises within the consciousnesses of individual Christians, and exists for them alone.

It is time to specify some of these important questions. They are such for Christians; it is crucial to realize this. For example, if in a conversation the Christian finds himself unable to explain the congruence between his belief in a God who is creator, and a theory of evolution which seems to make that belief obsolete, there is a problem. But the problem is not acute for the person who refuses to believe that there is a God who created all things out of nothing. It is the Christian's problem. It is this kind of experience of frustration, difficult to describe precisely, with which we are dealing. The new apologetic seeks to discover the causes for the presence of this inability to integrate, this disintegration, and to outline a reasonable matrix as a basis for a solution.

After formulating different questions and attempting to probe their significance, I will attempt to show why, historically, the questions have arisen and how, though they are different in form, they reflect the same basic problems.

4. CHRISTIANS AND HUMANISTS

The first series of questions arises in a variety of contexts. These questions ask the difference between the values professed by

Christians in their faith, and those lived out by so many unbelievers. An example which I have used elsewhere is that of two
persons working in the Peace Corps in, let us say, a country in
Central America. One, who happens to be a Christian, works
daily alongside his colleague, building huts, teaching in the
school, and generally helping the people in the village. His
colleague, who refers to himself as a humanist, performs the
same tasks, working just as diligently in service of the villagers.
In getting to know each other and in discussing religious faith
and human principles, a serious question arises in the mind of
the Christian as the result of his friend's persistent inquiries. Is
there anything about Christianity which he can offer to his friend,
which will improve the life of the latter?

Christ taught his apostles to pray; he also commanded them to
go and teach all men, baptizing them. How do prayers contribute
to the work in the village? What does the Christian have to offer
to his friend besides a belief in a God who is supernatural and
exists beyond the borders of sense experience? What can he urge
besides a moral code based upon the commandments of this God,
and a hopeful belief in some kind of immortality as a reward
for good works here below? The humanist might very well feel
that Christian faith offers him nothing of value. It offers him,
in fact, a more selfish motive for doing what he is already doing:
loving persons. At present he is dedicating himself for two years
to selfless labor in Central America because of a commitment to
humanity. Would Christian faith have him believe that his good
deeds will gain him heavenly recompense as well as human gratitude? If so, would it not provide him with a more selfish motive?
He loves other persons simply because they are human beings,
not because they have been created in God's image, or because
God has threatened him with eternal pain if he refuses to love
them.

The problem of faith, note, is not the humanist's. It is a
serious question in the mind of the Christian. When he thinks
about his faith, about what he believes as a Christian, he finds it

exceedingly difficult to understand how it is intrinsically related to the kind of life he now leads—except insofar as it is Christ's teaching that charitable service of human beings is meritorious. For human beings have been created in God's image. When the Christian thinks of faith, he recalls the Nicene Creed, which he recites each Sunday:

> I believe in one God, the Father almighty, maker of heaven and earth, and of all things visible and invisible. And I believe in one Lord, Jesus Christ, the only-begotten Son of God; born of the Father before all ages; God of God, Light of Light, true God of true God. Begotten, not made, of one substance with the Father. By whom all things were made. Who for us men and for our salvation came down from heaven. And he became flesh by the Holy Spirit of the Virgin Mary; and was made man. He was crucified for us, suffered under Pontius Pilate, and was buried. And on the third day he rose again, according to the Scriptures. He ascended into heaven and sits at the right hand of the Father. He will come again in glory to judge the living and the dead. And of his kingdom there will be no end. And I believe in the Holy Spirit, the Lord and Giver of life, who proceeds from the Father and the Son. Who together with the Father and the Son is adored and glorified, and who spoke through the prophets. And one holy, Catholic, and Apostolic Church. I confess one baptism for the forgiveness of sins, and I await the resurrection of the dead. And the life of the world to come. Amen.

How do God the Father, God the Son and God the Holy Spirit make a practical difference in the life of the Peace Corps worker, except as objects of prayer and sacramental worship? And what of the other elements in the Christian's profession of faith: the Catholic Church, baptism, the resurrection of the dead and the life of the world to come? Does not his faith, instead of relating him to the work he is performing, direct his attention beyond his work, to another world, the world of the supernatural?

Does not that otherworldliness provide the basis for his friend's judgment that Christian faith makes the believer a second-rate citizen of this world—here temporarily, but only for the sake of achieving eternal unity with God in the hereafter? The Christian may feel that such an accusation rests upon a caricature of his faith. But that does not solve the problem. How can a God-centered and heaven-centered faith be germane to human life? What can Christian faith add to the "natural" faith of the humanist? Perhaps Christ exaggerated the necessity for preaching the truths he taught. Perhaps he simply was unaware of the fact that two thousand years later so many individuals could live lovingly in service of other men without religious beliefs.

For the Christian to refer semijokingly to his friend as an "anonymous Christian" does not really solve the problem either. Besides patronizing his friend by refusing to allow him the privilege of refusing to believe in God, there is another difficulty. If anonymous Christianity is sufficient for his friend, though it does not oblige him to conform to Christianity's legal requirements, sacramental and spiritual exercises and moral prohibitions, why are those requirements, prohibitions and exercises important to anyone?

Most Christians do not serve in the Peace Corps. But they often encounter the same question in their own lives: What difference does Christianity make? The Christian who is unable to respond to his own satisfaction to that question often comes to the realization that his religion has meaning only as describing a small compartment in his life in which he stores his unanswerable questions concerning God and death. He realizes how he has been able to live most of his life without even being aware of his inability to reconcile his religion with that life.

The "Sunday Christian" is a creature much more in evidence than the Peace Corps worker. He is berated incessantly from the pulpits of parish churches. It is he who is able consistently to separate what he does for one hour each week from what he does during the rest of the week. For that one hour he is religious, pays homage to God and Christ, contributes a percentage of his salary to the collection and joins with his fellow worshipers in condemning the biblical Pharisees because of their hypocrisy. He is the "respectable" citizen who has wreaked so much damage by his ability to keep his Christian principles isolated in the religious sphere of life. Monsignor Paul Hanley Furfey, in his book *The Respectable Murderers*, makes the point driven home by Bonhoeffer during World War II in Nazi Germany: it is the "respectable" members of society who, through their failure to protest immoral policies undertaken by their governments, are morally responsible for those policies.[8]

How many Christians in this country make the facile distinction between moral and political issues, to avoid making a judgment concerning immoral governmental domestic and foreign policies? How many Catholic university students, utilizing the same distinction, lash out angrily at their so-called "hippie" fellow students' adoption of techniques of draft refusal and opposition to the selective service system? How many Christians in the United States are able sincerely to worship God and Christ in church on Sundays, while they ignore the social struggles of their black brothers and sisters, on "sociological" grounds? Why were Christians among the crowds in Milwaukee, Wisconsin, during the past two years, jeering and throwing bricks at Father Groppi and his fellow marchers for civil rights and equal employment opportunities for blacks?

Examples are numerous. Many Christians experience a deep frustration at their inability to integrate their faith with their lives. But it is even more tragic that many Christians fail to experience the frustration. Never having allowed themselves to ask the kinds of questions about their religious faith that they ask about "worldly" matters, they are more than content, consciously or unconsciously, to allow their Christian professions of faith to remain divorced from their social, professional and civic lives.

For the former, the frustrated Christian, there must be a new apologetic: a vision of faith which allows for the integration of which we have been speaking. For the latter, the contented

8 Paul H. Furfey, *The Respectable Murderers* (New York: Herder and Herder, 1966).

Christian, there must be a way to confront him with the gap between what his "Christian" label implies and the values by which he actually lives. It is too easy these days to call oneself Christian. Those who do, cannot be allowed to do so verbally alone.

So this first question, a problem for some Christians, regrettably not one for others, concerns the relationship between Christian faith and normal human life. What makes the problem in this form possible is the tendency to conceive faith as having essentially to do with God, religious institutions and an afterlife. The problem, in other words, arises largely from within the Christian tradition, because of the manner in which members of that tradition have learned to understand the contents of their faith.

5. FAITH AND SCIENTIFIC REASON

The second series of questions is related to the first. Like the preceding questions, they reflect different educational levels and various life situations. Generally expressed, the questions deal with the relationship between faith and reason. Is Christian faith in any way reasonable? Is it possible, really possible, to be intellectually honest about faith, to the degree that one can be rigorously demanding about scientific claims to knowledge and truth? Is faith by nature blind, centered exclusively on a supernatural God beyond sense perception? Is the answer to every serious question about faith the same—that it is a "mystery"? Are the claims of faith exempt completely from processes of verification? If not, why not? If so, what are the criteria for such verification?

How can a God completely beyond this world of experience be apprehended and spoken of in meaningful language? Is this kind of God not the "deus ex machina" spoken of by Bonhoeffer and others, the God whose decreasingly important function is to answer the questions as yet unanswered by science? Is this God not the one who has been pushed out of men's lives gradually, as natural and social sciences have been able to account for human life in "natural" terms?

These questions resolve themselves into one: Do the claims of Christian faith admit in any way of the kind of reasonable analysis to which all other human claims to knowledge are susceptible? Or is it true that the faith of the believer is indeed an isolated spiritual treasure, to be guarded against the demonic assaults of natural reason? Are Christians given religious answers to be memorized, before they have serious questions?

The relationship between these questions and the first series of questions should be evident. For if a concept of faith is conceived as totally God-centered and heaven-centered, otherworldly, then the human wisdom and analytic powers of this world do not apply. It is not that Christians really believe faith to be *un*reasonable. It is that faith, as a supernatural gift from God, is above or beyond the operations of reason.

Christians who are frustrated because of their inability to integrate their religious faith with their lives, unable to answer for themselves the question of the relevance of faith, are those for whom the relationship between faith and reason is an important issue. They may have studied somewhat in the fields of history, philosophy and literature. They may know something of the historical opposition by churchmen to the advances of the natural and social sciences. They are forced to acknowledge an accommodation in Christian teaching about creation during the past one hundred years, largely because of the contributions of scientists such as Galileo, Newton and Darwin.

As evidence accumulated against the likelihood that the human race has descended from a single pair of human beings, Adam and Eve, the theory which expresses that position, monogenism, has become increasingly tenuous. Present research favors rather the theory of polygenism, that is, that mankind in its present state has evolved from small groups of ancestors. Christians know of the resistance offered by their Christian teachers and theologians to the acceptance of the theory of evolution itself. And the feeling emerges within them that there is a basic incompatibility between faith and science, between revealed truth and the discoveries of human reason.

At the same time, they live in a culture which reflects an increasing respect for the methods of science and a firm confidence in the ability of scientific research and engineering to eradicate most of the evils in human life.[9] Believers are not surprised to learn of the existence of scientific atheists, unbelievers claiming a permanent opposition between scientific knowledge and religious faith. For, if the truth be told, many educated Christians sense the same opposition, secretly feeling that if they allowed their minds the freedom to proceed with rigorous rational scrutiny of their faith, they too would be forced to reject it. Thus they use their toasters and electric toothbrushes, watch their television sets, observe men circumnavigate and tread upon the moon, and suppress their curiosity to learn more about the scientific advances which make it all possible. Too many profess a faith whose actual basis is ignorance—faith in God made possible by the gaps in scientific knowledge.

The social sciences as well have caused problems for religion. During the past century especially, psychology and sociology have emerged as bodies of knowledge more deserving of the title "science," as their methods for empirical evaluation of data have improved. Names like Sigmund Freud, Theodore Reik, John Watson, B. F. Skinner, Max Weber and Emile Durkheim are associated with what some refer to as the demise of religious faith.[10]

Can religious faith be shown by psychologists to have its roots in the human wish for fulfillment, a wish born of the inability to face life as it is? If "God" refers to an imaginary being, created

9 Cf. Robert Adolfs, The Grave of God, trans. N. D. Smith (New York: Harper & Row, 1967), pp. 78–81.

10 Cf. Thomas O'Dea, Sociology of Religion (Englewood Cliffs, N.J.: Prentice-Hall, 1966), for a clear and interesting account and evaluation of social and psychological challenges to the viability of religious faith in general. Our purpose in these pages is indicative; a thorough examination of the issues to which we point is outside the scope of the present work. Suggested readings in this area will be offered in Chapter Five.

and then served by men to explain what they cannot as yet explain themselves, then the viability of religious faith is questionable, to say the least. If man's capacity to exercise genuine freedom and creativity in his life is an illusion, shown to be so by the experiments of behavioral psychologists in the field of bioengineering, then any religious basis for teachings concerning moral responsibility is tenuous. If the major religious traditions of mankind can be traced back to their origins in primitive animism and totemism, accounted for by social psychologists in terms of mass neurosis, is there not indeed an irreducible opposition between scientific knowledge and religious faith? If sociologists can demonstrate through statistics the complex manners by which societies generate religious beliefs to enable the haves to exploit the have-nots, are not the claims of religious faith to transcendental truth destroyed?

If the preceding questions seem to be slanted purposely in order to heighten their effect, it does not alter the fact that those questions, in just those forms, exist for a great many Christians. As we will see later, most philosophers of religion no longer consider such questions unanswerable. But they remain so for too many Christians, many of whom experience, whether or not they should, a gnawing fear that science is destroying the possibilities for religious belief.

A more sophisticated version of the same problem, arising from certain presuppositions about the claims of scientific knowledge to truth and certitude, is the problem of religious language. Philosophers of religion and of language have contributed many treatises to this topic during the past forty years, making the possibility of religious language, including talk about God, an important issue. One of the best ways to indicate the difficulty involved is to refer to the famous parable of the philosopher John Wisdom.[11]

11 John Hick, ed., "Gods," in *Readings in the Philosophy of Religion* (Englewood Cliffs, N.J.: Prentice-Hall, 1964), pp. 413–28.

Two men come upon a clearing in the forest. One of them, a religious believer, noticing some plants and flowers among the grass and trees, considers the clearing to be a garden. The other, a skeptic, noticing the disarray caused by weeds among the flowers, disagrees. He claims that the clearing is nothing more than that—a random clearing. After some discussion, the two decide to resolve the issue by awaiting the return of the gardener, if indeed there be one. After a long time, during which they arrange signals and set up warning devices to alert them should the gardener appear during their sleeping hours, it becomes impractical to wait any longer. The skeptic, confident that his original claim has been verified, is surprised to find his friend still unwilling to abandon his belief that there is a gardener. The believer argues that, even though they have not seen or sensed the gardener in any way, his original claim has not been falsified. For the gardener is invisible and insensible. Frustrated, his friend wonders how such a gardener differs from an imaginary gardener, or from none at all.

Thus, the parable seems to say, believers and unbelievers observe the same world and live in it together. Believers, in the face of evidence from the natural and social sciences, persist in claiming to know that there exists an invisible and insensible God beyond the world. The existence of evil and suffering, which confirms the inability of unbelievers to reconcile reality as it is with a God who is good, seems to make no difference at all to the claims of believers. In fact, religious persons are known to experience a strengthening of their faith, rather than a diminishing, in extended encounters with suffering in themselves and others.

To paraphrase a common example illustrating this point, consider a man on a crowded downtown street. Standing with a friend, he notices a pedestrian narrowly avoid a collision with a bus. He remarks to his friend that such incidents strengthen his conviction that there does indeed exist a God whose nature is goodness. For the pedestrian could have been killed.

Minutes later both men are amazed to witness the same pedestrian, again confronting a bus in the street. This time, however, he is not spry enough. He is hit by the bus and knocked to the pavement. Unhurt, he manages to gain his feet after a time and make his way into a nearby store. The believer, reading his friend's thoughts, finds his conviction about the existence of a good God unshaken by the event which has just occurred. Why? Because, obviously, the man could have been killed: he was spared a horrible death by God.

One hour later, after having witnessed the luckless pedestrian's futile attempt to cross the street once more, an attempt which resulted tragically in his demise, the believer can be heard giving voice to his renewed faith in God. For God, in his goodness, has deigned to call the pedestrian to a happier life, freeing him from a suffering existence in this vale of tears.

Nothing which occurs weakens or challenges the believer's faith in God. Is it surprising that his friend accuses him of maintaining an irrational belief? Yet he is able, somehow, to believe, in the face of contrary evidence.

Partly because of the dissatisfaction with the claims of believers about God, claims which seemed oblivious to the evidence, rules concerning the meaningfulness of human discourse soon emerged. Proceeding from a confidence in the degree of certitude present in the scientific method, philosophers began to suggest certain criteria which language must fulfill to be meaningful.

Ludwig Wittgenstein, Rudolf Carnap, Susan Stebbins, Gilbert Ryle and Alfred Ayer are names associated with the establishment of rules for meaningful discourse.[12] Soon after 1934 the phrase "principle of verification" appeared and became well known. This principle was an attempt to outline criteria for language. For a statement to be meaningful, it must be empirically verifiable, mathematically tautological, or logically consistent.

Empirical verification seemed to be an excellent criterion. For

[12] Suggested readings for Chapter One are included in this book.

it demanded that language be anchored, no matter how indirectly, in concrete reality. Words should refer to things, not to other words. In normal human discourse, for example, the statement, "There is a painting by Modigliani in my room," is meaningful because it can be either verified or falsified by a trip to my room. At this point the issue is not whether the statement is true or false, but whether it is meaningful. If, when we get to my room, the painting is not in fact present, I am a liar. But at least I make sense: my statement is tied to concrete reality, and has been falsified. "The moon is made of green cheese" is a statement which is no longer meaningful, as it was for hundreds of years. Now that we possess an actual chunk of the moon, the statement is not, in principle, verifiable or falsifiable. We have the evidence, and the issue is decided.

These qualities of verifiability and falsifiability make scientific statements among the most meaningful. For the method of science, by definition, includes not only theory and hypothesis, but the process of empirical verification.

Mathematical statements are meaningful because in the last analysis the terms on the right side of the equal sign are another way of "saying" the terms on the left side. $2 + 2 = 1 + 3$. A similar observation can be made concerning logic. If $a = b$, and $b = c$; then $a = c$. The terms are definable; the major and minor premises stand adequate; and the conclusion can be demonstrated.

The main threat to religious language came from the first part of the verification principle: empirical verifiability. The strength of that criterion is its foundation in common sense. It requires that words refer to concrete realities. A word such as "God," which by definition refers to a reality in no way concrete, becomes therefore meaningless. And the debate between believers and unbelievers about God's existence becomes a fruitless one. "God is good" is a statement unverifiable and unfalsifiable through ordinary methods of providing evidence. Therefore it is neither true nor false, but meaningless.

This denial that religious language is meaningful has been beneficial to theologians and to religious persons in general. Theology has a tendency to become abstract and unintelligible to earthlings, as Dr. John Macquarrie has said.[13] One of the most common and serious complaints among students in theology classes at Catholic universities is the theoretical nature of the lectures of their instructors.

In an effort to safeguard a place and function for religious language, while essentially accepting the principle of verification, some philosophers developed "noncognitive" theories. If statements concerning God are not claims to cognition or knowledge or truth, then there is no problem. In other words, instead of attempting to find rules governing discourse about God which is really language referring to a supernatural being, these functionalist philosophers interest themselves in the study of religion insofar as it is a human phenomenon. What is important is the function which religion exercises in individual life and in social institutions. Religious language, then, becomes meaningful because it does not claim cognitive content, but reveals an attitude or value in the heart of the speaker. So "God loves his people" is a meaningful statement because it really means, "I feel loved and protected with other members in this religious community." It is not important whether or not the statement actually refers to God. At least it is meaningful.

This particular aspect of the discussion is the subject of many careful treatments. For present purposes, it is enough to indicate that a "solution" of the problem in terms of noncognitive functionalism is no solution at all. A believer could not possibly accept the kind of ultimate demands his faith makes of him, and remain oblivious to whether those beliefs are true or false. Believers necessarily claim that their beliefs are true. Otherwise,

[13] John Macquarrie, *God-Talk* (New York: Harper & Row, 1967). Cf. also Eric L. Mascall, *Existence and Analogy* (London: Darton, Longman and Todd, Ltd., 1949); and Ian T. Ramsey, *Religious Language* (New York: Macmillan, 1963).

why believe them? The only possible religious stance would then be agnosticism, colored by pretense: although I do not know whether my beliefs are true, nonetheless I will live as if they are. The noncognitive "solution" could be a real answer only for an unbeliever, outside any community of faith. To expect a religious person to live in a certain way because of his faith, and to inform him simultaneously that he should be indifferent as to whether what he believes is true or false, is to be unrealistic. There is a serious problem in this area of religious language. It must be acknowledged, not sidestepped.

These are some of the ways in which the second series of questions, concerning the reasonableness of Christian faith, arises today for the believer. These questions arise for many in the form of a hazy fear that the progress of science makes faith intellectually untenable. They are present in others as the result of some reading and study in psychology or sociology, in the feeling that religion can be accounted for in nonreligious ways. Others find themselves confused by the complicated debate concerning the meaningfulness of religious language. The result is that there are many educated Christians whose understanding of faith does not admit evidence or sense experience of any kind to be considered, because of the fear that faith cannot support the burden of rational analysis.

The problem does not disappear after they study natural theology, or the philosophy of God. The believer knows his faith to be a gift, centered on a supernatural being. He is thus disposed to acknowledge that natural, reasonable knowledge of God is not identical with faith. A God reached through reasonable argument remains impersonal. He is described as first mover, final cause, or that greater than which nothing can be conceived.

The God of religious faith is personal. The believer calls God "Father," and thanks him for the gift of faith, which is a genuine gift, not the result of a rational demonstration. He may sense, moreover, that if his faith were so compatible with reason, he would have to consider all unbelievers to be unreasonable. They are not.

The arguments for the existence of God on the basis of reason, designed to demonstrate that existence to the unbeliever, formed part of the old apologetic. The problem faced by the new apologetic still remains: How do Christians, given their profession of faith in divine Revelation, relate faith and reason as claims to knowledge and truth? Relatively uninterested in demonstrating the truths of faith to unbelievers, such Christians find themselves frustrated by their own inability to integrate their understanding of faith with their normal reliance on the methods of reason.

To attempt this integration, then, is a task oriented toward the psychological experience of believers. Such an attempt does not consist in creating caricatures of atheistic and agnostic positions, then attacking them in such a way as to vindicate the beliefs of Christians. Its purpose is to indicate the serious problems confronting believers, problems in the forms in which they are actually encountered. It includes the attempt to speak meaningfully to provide a vision of Christian faith which does not allow for the lack of integration we have been discussing. The problems exist for Christians. They alone can and must resolve them.

6. OTHER FAITHS

The third series of questions indicating the difficulty in reconciling faith with life has to do with the religious beliefs of other men. This is another way in which the question of the intrinsic reasonableness and relevance of Christian Revelation to human life becomes acute for many believers.

Does my Christian profession of faith, by which I believe what the Church teaches to be true, require that I refuse to allow myself to become interested in the beliefs of Hindus and Buddhists? Do I know beforehand that what they believe is false? Should I attempt to convert them to my own faith?

Why, after studying the traditions of other religious persons, and having recognized therein some values not present, at least in the same way, in the Christian traditions, should I remain a Christian? Are not all religions simply different ways of saying the same thing? Should I be concerned at the resistance to Christianity encountered by missionaries in foreign lands? What benefit does Christianity bring to the people in those countries? Should I be upset to learn that the percentage of Christians among the religions of the world is decreasing, while other religious traditions, such as Islam, reflect growing memberships?

The days of the "ostrich" approach to Christian faith are gone. Ignoring the issue is not the solution. While it may have been possible for some in the past to practice their Christianity with only a faint awareness of the existence in faraway lands of pagans who were destined one day to be baptized by missionaries, it is no longer possible. Transportation, communications, education: modern technology is expanding the borders of our religious awareness as well as our political and social awareness. The future history of the world will include persons of all religious faiths, as well as those of no faith at all.

Dr. Wilfred Cantwell Smith is one scholar who has argued cogently that future political and economic relationships with the East must include concomitant interest in, and understanding of, Oriental religious traditions.[14] The ability to separate and conceptualize "religion" as a thing, one element among many which constitute a culture, seems to be a particularly Western ability. Westerners can establish economic relationships with other countries, and totally prescind from all consideration of religious traditions. As we noticed earlier, American Christians can act politically during the week, and religiously for an hour on Sundays. But there are peoples whose language does not even contain a word to translate our term "religion": no such thing

[14] Wilfred Cantwell Smith, *The Faith of Other Men* (New York: Mentor, 1965), Introduction.

exists, separable from the other elements in their lives. Such people, when they are acting politically, are also acting religiously. Though religion can easily be compartmentalized, both theoretically and practically, by many Western believers, this is often not the case in Eastern lands.

The kind of arrogance which has characterized the approach of Western Christianity to Eastern faiths is analogous to that sometimes present in governmental programs of economic assistance. An example of the first kind of arrogance is the practice of some Roman Catholic elementary school students, who "buy 'pagan babies'" for five dollars each. For that sum they have the right to bestow a name on a small foreign child. Though these students are not culpably arrogant, they would themselves undoubtedly be shocked to learn that foreign children were buying them.

An indication of the political arrogance is the Communist charge that America demonstrates materialism in its foreign aid programs with Asian citizens. Money pours in from Uncle Sam without any corresponding appreciation for the religious sensibilities of the people. Few Americans familiarize themselves with the religious traditions of other peoples.

More Christians are coming to believe that the way a person lives is more important than what he proclaims to believe. "Baptism of desire" is one phrase by which Roman Catholics account for the high quality of the moral lives of persons who have never encountered Christianity. They are equivalently baptized by their implicit desire to be saved, manifest in the high moral caliber of their lives.

If this kind of baptism suffices for salvation in the cases of others, and if it is impractical to imagine the day when the entire human race will give allegiance to the papacy, then why be a Catholic Christian? What difference does Christianity make to the lives of persons in Eastern religious traditions? Should missionaries continue to attempt to preach the gospel in foreign lands? If not, then Christianity is not necessary to all men. If it is not, it cannot be absolutely necessary to any. If, on the other hand, it is necessary, why do so many people refuse to accept it?

These questions, then, like the others, arise in the minds of Christians. Their primary concern is not the conversion of persons of other faiths, but the value of their own faith to persons in other religious traditions. Because the future of the world will in fact include Catholics, Protestants, Hindus, Buddhists, Moslems and Jews, it would seem to be a practical necessity to build up an atmosphere allowing for healthy communications. Christians must approach such communications in their own lives with an answer to the question: How does my profession of faith integrate my own life and relate to the lives of others?

"Rapidation" refers to the necessity in today's technological society for anticipating and preparing for the results of important human decisions years before their implementation.[15] These decisions will be made. Like all decisions, they will reflect certain values and principles. Christians must be able to understand why the principles of their faith are necessary. In other words, as Fr. Robert Adolfs has pointed out, the future will be the result of certain decisions which determine the lives of entire masses of human beings. Not only do these decisions concern air and water pollution, regulation of air space and nuclear proliferation. They include the ways in which computers are to be used in genetic regulation, and the criteria to be utilized in medicine for determining the difference between life and death in organ transplants. When the Christian claims that the principles of his faith are most adequate to inform those important decisions, he must be prepared to explain why. He must also be able to speak meaningfully of their importance to men of other religious faiths and to those of no religious faith at all. Why is the Nicene Creed so important, anyway?

These are serious questions for the reflective Christian. Is his faith in God relevant to a world populated by agnostic humanists,

[15] Adolfs, *op. cit.*, pp. 44–46.

scientists and persons of other religious traditions? Is his faith exhausted in the Nicene Creed? How can a religious faith which is God-centered, concerned with a supernatural reality, and heaven-centered, really be integrated with an honest acceptance of the necessity for living in the world? It is a problem for the Christian before it is one for the non-Christian.

7. INSTITUTIONAL CHRISTIAN FORMS

The last series of questions arising in various contexts, but indicating the same basic problem, concerns the institutional forms of Christianity. Most Christians find themselves in institutional communities or churches. For example, consider the members of the Roman Catholic Church, one which has proclaimed itself to be in the process of painful renewal. Is this institutional community as important to the world as it claims to be? Does not the presence of so much confusion and corruption in the institutional structures belie the claims of the Church to truth?

The Catholic today is observing and participating in one of the most prolific eras of self-criticism ever within his Church. Daniel Callahan and John L. McKenzie, among many others, have contrasted the ideals of love and community lived in the early Christian community with the indifference to personal values present in today's Church.[16]

Perhaps the recent worldwide reaction to Pope Paul VI's encyclical on birth control, *Humanae Vitae,* points up the problem most poignantly for all Catholics. It is impossible to have lived during the months immediately following the promulgation of that encyclical, and to have failed to notice the upheaval it occasioned throughout the Church. The encyclical was the occasion for the upheaval, not the cause. The theological discussions and

16 Daniel Callahan, *Honesty in the Church* (New York: Scribner, 1965); and John L. McKenzie, *Authority in the Church* (New York: Sheed & Ward, 1966).

debates concerning birth control morality which have ensued are not new. They simply emphasize and bring to the surface some of the serious questions which have been in the minds of reflective Catholics for many years.

The strongest disappointment for many Catholics has to do with the decision itself. Coming after the end of Vatican II and the publication of documents rich in biblical theology and personalistic insights, the encyclical seems to demonstrate an insensitivity to the realities of married life that is, in a sense, inexcusable. The disappointment becomes more acute with the realization that the Pope disregarded the recommendations of hundreds of doctors, sociologists and professionals, as well as the strong recommendations of the majority of his own commission. That commission was composed not only of clerics, but of competent and intelligent laymen from countries all over the world. The conclusion of the encyclical seems to disregard the economic and psychological hardships of so many married people.

The encyclical teaches that every marital act must be open to the transmission of life. Does this not betray a view of marital sex which is abstracted from the context of married love? In other words, does it not concentrate on the physical components of the action, showing little appreciation for the human context of love in which the action occurs? Is the human marital act not more rich and meaningful than the sexual activities of animals? How can the Catholic Church speak with genuine authority in this area? These are some of the questions being asked. How is the Catholic institutional form of Christianity relevant to the real life-situations of Catholics—or to those of other men and women?

The encyclical has also provided the occasion for many Catholics to observe the seeming insensitivity of some bishops toward priests in their dioceses. In many large cities, bishops who had signed their names to the documents of Vatican II, pledging themselves to maintain open and mature relationships with their priests, have failed to do so. Whether the criticism in all cases is justified or not, priests in this country continue their exodus from their ministries, partly because they claim that the ecclesiastical institution enslaves rather than liberates them.

From still another point of view, as Father John McKenzie has pointed out, many Catholics are scandalized by the loss of prestige suffered by their Church with regard to social issues. Their Church has appeared during this century to be more concerned with sexual morality than with implementing the high ideals of economic justice urged in the social encyclicals of Leo XIII and Paul VI. Catholics in Central America manifest indifference or hostility toward the Church because of its insensitivity to the plight of the poor and oppressed, and because of its lack of sympathy for the revolutions taking place.

The debate concerning the viability of the Catholic ecclesial institutions waxes strong in theological books and journals these days. The international wire services have acquainted their readers with the decision of Charles Davis, the prominent English Catholic theologian, to leave the Catholic priesthood and the Church, weary of the constricting nature of the institution. Some Catholics are confusedly aware of the disciplining of other theologians in recent years, including Herbert McCabe, Robert Adolfs, Hans Küng and Edward Schillebeeckx. They are becoming more disposed to accept as true the complaints of priests about the surreptitious banishments to which they or their colleagues have been subjected.

In still another context the value of the institutional Church is questioned: the religious ceremonies of daily and weekly life. The liturgical renewal may be occurring effectively in some areas of the country. But Catholics elsewhere are experiencing a disappointment in their discovery that the Mass can be just as dry and uninspiring in English, accompanied by a few hymns, as it was in Latin. Compounding the frustration are the books which appear, rejoicing at the progress of the Catholic reformation. These books are performing an invaluable service. In describing the process of renewal which should be taking place, they intensify the frustration and impatience of Catholics with the failure of renewal in their own parishes.

The Pope, bishops, priests, doctrines, ceremonies, grade schools, religious orders: how are the "Catholic" things of life really pertinent to the world? And how should a Catholic assess the significance of the confusion prevalent in the Church today? To what extent is the Church an object of, or element in, his religious faith? How do institutional religious forms as such figure into the faiths of adult Christians?

8. FAITH AND REVELATION: 1850–1896

Some of the questions and frustrations discussed above arise because of an inaccurate understanding by both Christians and non-Christians of the concepts of faith and Revelation. A faith formally exhausted in the Nicene Creed, God-centered and otherworldly, cannot but disturb the psyches of Christians attempting to understand their importance to the world. If we can, in fact, demonstrate that at least some of those questions owe their peculiar urgency to an inadequate understanding of what their faith really claims to know and what their God has revealed, then we can attempt to describe the central teachings of Christian Revelation in a way which will allow for the kind of integration between revealed faith and the world of men that is too often absent.

Part of the solution to the problem lies in the recognition that, despite the new language and emphases of the documents of the Second Vatican Council, such as the *Constitution on Divine Revelation,* many Catholics' understanding of the concepts of faith and Revelation is essentially that verbalized during the latter half of the nineteenth century.

Four documents which appeared during that time have exerted a strong influence on Catholics' approach to the concept of faith ever since. These are: the encyclical *Qui Pluribus,* by Pius IX, written in 1846; the encyclical *Satis Cogitum* of Leo XIII, appearing in 1896; and the two constitutions from the First Vatican Council in 1870, the *Constitution on the Church,* and the *Constitution on Faith.*[17]

Because Catholic teachings have nearly always emerged as a reaction to heretical challenges to orthodoxy within the Church, it is well to note briefly the presence of certain occasions for the Church's teachings in the nineteenth century concerning faith and Revelation. In general, the last half of that century witnessed the continuation of the ascent of the methods of natural science to a position of general respectability, as well as the evolution of the social sciences, psychology and sociology. One reason for the Church's concern with the concepts of faith and Revelation was its position in a Western culture whose scientific advance could possibly challenge the validity of Christian faith. When science seemed to destroy or contradict the historical authenticity of biblical accounts, was Christian Revelation itself in peril?

Within the Church there emerged two kinds of responses to the challenge, later to be designated as rationalism and fideism.[18] Some Christians, rationalists, were fearful of allowing an ineradicable opposition between faith and reason to develop. They taught that the truths of Christian Revelation are not only not incompatible with human reason, but are so compatible with it that they can be derived through the processes of natural reason. Fideists, on the other hand, solicitous to safeguard the gratuity of divine Revelation—the necessity to understand it as a gift from God, unattainable through mere human effort—emphasized its supernatural nature and object. Instead of the proximity between reason and revealed truth, they emphasized the difference between natural and supernatural modes of knowing. In doing so,

[17] These documents are contained in English in William Kelly *et al., The Church Teaches* (St. Louis: B. Herder, 1964), pp. 11–41 and pp. 67–80.

[18] For the proponents of this position consult Kelly, *ibid.;* for the present purpose it is sufficient merely to indicate their existence and general nature.

they came quite close to maintaining that the gift of faith really has nothing to do with the processes of human reason.

The magisterium or teaching authority of the Church, the Pope in union with the bishops, thus found itself with the task of articulating definitions of faith and Revelation which avoided the extremes of both rationalism and fideism. In *Qui Pluribus,* Pius IX set the tone and forged some of the language for the solemn teachings which were soon to evolve. Against the rationalists, he emphasized that the Catholic faith gets all its power from the authority of the God who has spoken; and that it could never be deduced or completed by human reason. Revelation is true, not because its truth is recognized by the light of natural reason, but because God can neither deceive nor be deceived (D. 1636).[19]

Against the Fideists, the Pope attempted to vindicate the necessary role of reason in the activity of faith. Human reason, he taught, has a restricted function: it should inquire into divine Revelation with care, making certain that God has indeed spoken, and paying him service.

> For, although faith is above reason, it is impossible to discover real opposition or disagreement between them; because faith and reason originate from the same source of immutable and eternal truth, God, who is great and good; and they are helpful to one another . . . (D. 1635).

Catholics were asked to hold together in their minds the two-faceted belief that, although faith is centered on God and therefore is not completely accessible to reason, it does not in any way conflict with the activities of reason.

Furthermore, the truths of the supernatural order of faith must be protected and promulgated by Christian "soldiers."

> With the crucifix alone as its standard, the Church of Christ has spread over the whole world, on land and sea, from East to West. It has eliminated the basic errors of idolatry, destroyed the clouds of

[19] References are to Denzinger's *Enchiridion Symbolorum,* the source book for Catholic teaching.

error, conquered all kinds of enemies. It has subjected to Christ's sweet yoke all peoples, no matter how barbaric and cruel, no matter how different as far as natural customs, laws and institutions (D. 1638).

So the Catholic Church, as guardian of the revealed truths of God whose source is God himself, is commissioned to enlighten all people who are in error, either because they are idolaters or because they happen to be different.

As late as 1896, Leo XIII, in *Satis Cogitum*, spoke from the same frame of reference, when he taught that Christ willed the establishment of only one Church in the world. Because the Catholic Church alone has been founded by Christ, no other faith or church can be true. Consequently, Catholics have a solemn duty to support missionary endeavors whose purpose is the eradication of religious error in the world (D. 1954).

The encyclicals during these years reflected the approach taken by the magisterium during the First Vatican Council in the constitutions on faith and Revelation. These latter documents, products of an ecumenical council, are far more significant.

In the document on faith, after teaching that God can be known with certainty by the light of natural reason from the things that he has created, the bishops of Vatican I emphasized that Revelation is nonetheless necessary, because man is destined to an end which is supernatural, not natural (D. 1786). The distinction between faith and reason is made clearly and often. They are two orders of knowledge, distinct in origin and object (D. 1795).

"Distinct in origin and object": this is a key phrase, replete with significance. For, although the fathers included remarks about the lack of real conflict between faith and reason, Catholics born during the next one hundred years were to grow up learning in religion classes that when "natural" reason reaches its limits, then the supernatural virtue of faith takes over to provide understanding of the inner nature of God.

This is an important insight. Although the formal statements themselves presupposed rather sophisticated neoscholastic distinctions, the necessary distinctions have not found their way into the minds of Catholics since. It matters little that the statements themselves do not urge an absolute gap between faith and reason. They have been interpreted as doing so.

The Catholic born since the time of Vatican I, paradoxically, finds himself urged, in discussions with unbelievers, to develop many lucid and reasonable arguments that the Christian religion is divine and that it finds the origin of its dogmas in the Lord (D. 1638). He is taught to believe that this truth is demonstrated by the birth, life and Resurrection of Jesus Christ, the predictions of the prophets, the splendor of the miracles recorded in Scripture, the constancy of the martyrs and the glory of the saints of God—all specifically suprarational evidence. As a proof for the superiority of the Catholic Church among all religions in the world, the Catholic learns that the Church itself is a great and perpetual motive of credibility, an irrefutable proof of its own divine mission (D. 1794).

To the Catholic Church comes the same title to the allegiance of men as to God himself. In the *Constitution on the Church* the basis for that allegiance appears, verbalized in the dogma of papal infallibility:

> . . . the Roman Pontiff, when he speaks *ex cathedra,* that is, when he is fulfilling the office of Pastor and Teacher of all Christians, on his supreme Apostolical authority, he defines a doctrine concerning faith or morals to be held by the Universal Church; by means of the divine assistance promised him in blessed Peter, he is endowed with that infallibility with which the Divine Redeemer has willed that his Church—in defining doctrine concerning faith or morals—should be equipped. Therefore, such definitions of the Roman Pontiff are, of themselves, irreformable. If anyone shall presume (God forbid) to contradict this our definition, let him be anathema (D. 1839).

The manner in which many Catholic Christians think about Revelation and faith reflects the approaches underlying the preceding documents. Catechisms and books on Catholic dogma embody the same basic approach, not yet replaced by the new theology, or the documents of Vatican II. It is this approach to faith, centered on God and obsessed with the divinity of the Church, which is largely responsible for the serious questions discussed during the first part of the chapter. For these indicate, as we saw, the inability of many Christians to integrate their faith with reasonable human experience.

In a popular source book of Catholic teachings, first printed in 1955, we read the following: Revelation is

> . . . the positive act of communication, by which the Creator makes known to the creature the religious truth he intends to reveal. . . . The divine communication is something supernatural, not merely as an event that takes place outside of the ordinary, natural course of events, but also in its contents; because the principal revealed truths so far exceed the ability of natural reason that the latter cannot discover or fully understand them.[20]

Are the "contents" of Revelation outside the natural course of events? What course of events could this be? And what is its relevance to the normal course of events? Whether or not the Church in the nineteenth century actually taught a position smacking of fideism, the way in which some Christians understand their faith today is confusedly fideistic. It is this misunderstanding which contributes to the consternation at being unable to integrate their faith with their life in the world within the natural course of events. Students in religious education classes still learn that faith is the virtue by which we believe truths about God because he has revealed them, not because those truths make sense. They make their own kind of sense, as demonstrated by reference to miraculous occurrences, outside the domain of nature. As these students become more educated, it is difficult for them not to continue feeling that religious truths exist in a realm of being all by themselves. Enter the questions of the humanist

20 Kelly, *op. cit.,* p. 11.

and the problem of religious language. It is only logical to expect that faith and its institutional expressions in churches should occupy restricted spheres of interest.

If the Nicene Creed does indeed exhaust the contents of Christian faith, then the concern of faith does center on a supernatural and transcendent God and an eternal life with him in a world beyond this one. The whole discussion of the value of Christian faith to the world of men is predetermined by limiting it to the issues of the existence of God and the life hereafter. Historically this has been the case. Immediately, upon raising the question of the relationship or pertinence of his faith to the humanist, for example, the Christian finds himself attempting either to argue about the existence of God or to defend the enterprise of discussing the topic at all. The dialogue between Christianity and atheism has been structured by defining the contents of Christian faith in terms of the question of the existence of God. The Christian often reaches a point at which he begins to share the frustrations of the person with whom he is speaking. He begins himself to wonder what a belief in a God-apart-from-the-world can add, practically, to the lives of men. The problem is the Christian's.

As Fr. John Courtney Murray has pointed out, many atheists and agnostics today have simply lost interest in arguments about God and the afterlife.[21] This loss of interest has resulted, largely, from the manner in which Christians themselves have described and isolated the claims of faith. For the discussion usually centers on a supernatural God. Both the Christian and the unbeliever accept the inbuilt invulnerability of the contents of faith to critical analysis—the unbeliever because he sees evidence as irrelevant to the discussion, the Christian because his faith is so far above the realm of reason. It is simply presupposed that the discussion about the practical value of Christianity in the world turns on the issue of the existence or nonexistence of a totally

21 Cf. John C. Murray, *The Problem of God* (New Haven: Yale University Press, 1964), pp. 101–20.

transcendent God apprehended by the supernatural virtue of faith. Because such discussions do not appeal to persons whose primary interest is in acting constructively in this world, they are often inconclusive.

Experience in teaching at Catholic high schools or universities reveals how strongly these presuppositions concerning the scope of Christian faith are present among the students. Students are frequently prepared to grant to their theology instructors a privilege they would never consider allowing their history or philosophy professors: that of taking refuge in mystery. They have been conditioned to presuppose that faith begins where reason ceases to function.

The same students who can become the most obsessed with arguments for and against the existence of a good God, can leave behind their faith as they pass from theology class to English literature, reinforcing their religious isolationism. Later, they can graduate from college to become "Sunday Christians," preserving the "religious" dimensions of their lives from the "secular." Their understanding of Christian faith, forged during their long years of religious education, has included that implicit semifideism, that feeling that faith is meant to be kept apart from the rules of critical analysis governing much of "normal life." There will come a time when, either in terms of the challenges which we have discussed, or in some other manner, that lack of integration (dis-integration) between faith and life will become painfully real for them: What difference does Christian faith make, anyway?

9. CONCLUSIONS

Concepts of faith and Revelation which are solely God-centered, presupposing an inbuilt governor on rational thought processes, are too narrow. They have proved their inadequacy to serious questions in our time, some of which we discussed earlier.

Two tendencies within the Christian community contribute to

the problem of faith. The first is the approach which informed the documents of Vatican Council I, an approach we have designed as the old apologetic. It was too narrowly rationalistic and lifeless, creating in Catholics the ability to separate their faith from their lives.

The second tendency, very much in evidence in our own day, is antirational. It rejects the old apologetic and attempts to present Christian faith and Revelation in a new way, frequently ignoring the necessity for Christians to understand the reasonableness of their faith. To reject the old apologetic must not be to reject this need for critical reflection concerning faith.

The pages of the New Testament tell of a man called Jesus whose faith was and continues to be redemptive for men. This man spoke simply, not only about God, but about human life in this world: the way it is, and the way it should be. He saw the world and human life in a manner uniquely his own. He maintained a degree of intimacy with God impossible for any other man. Yet his mission was the redemption of men. He saw and lived in this world, and he participated in human life. He still does. He taught and lived out the truth that the only way to attain true unity with his Father is to love men as brothers. He specified the meaning of that term "love" in his being, life, teachings and actions: "Greater love than this hath no man." That love must be operative in a man's life, he said, before that man can worship God.

There is a necessity, from within the Christian tradition, to articulate a concept of faith and of Revelation which will not limit and predetermine the discussion of the value of Christianity in the world. It must be a concept of faith which will clarify as it makes possible the integration of human life. Such a concept is important, not primarily to allow once again for the interesting arguments between believers and unbelievers; but to provide the kind of vision in terms of which the Christian can understand the value of his serious involvement in the affairs of this earth.

To live one's life and attempt to love men as brothers because God has commanded it, is to fail to understand what Christianity is all about. For what God has commanded makes sense.

The following chapters, then, include some suggestions for an expanded concept of faith, along with a discussion of some of the implications of such a concept.

10. SUGGESTED READINGS

Durkheim, Emile. *The Elementary Forms of the Religious Life,* trans. J. Swain. Glencoe, Ill: The Free Press, 1954.

Feuerbach, Ludwig. *The Essence of Christianity.* Trans. G. Eliot. New York: Harper, 1957.

Freud, Sigmund. *Civilization and Its Discontents.* Ed. & trans. J. Strachey. New York: Norton, 1961.

O'Dea, Thomas. *The Sociology of Religion.* Englewood Cliffs, N.J.: Prentice-Hall, 1966.

Parsons, Talcott. *Essays in Sociological Theory.* Glencoe, Ill: The Free Press, 1954.

Wach, Joachim. *The Sociology of Religion.* Chicago: University of Chicago Press, 1944.

Weber, Max. *The Sociology of Religion.* Trans. E. Fischoff. Boston: Beacon Press, 1963.

2:SUGGESTING AN ENRICHED CONCEPT OF FAITH

In this chapter I will suggest a description of faith which, it may be hoped, is more adequate to the richness of that gift for Christians. Such a description should provide a wider and more realistic matrix from which Christians can think and can integrate their religious experience of faith with their human experience. Christians' understanding of the nature and function of faith should not create the serious problems discussed in the preceding chapter. This is not to say that faith can be explained in such a manner as to dispel all questions. That is hardly desirable, even if it were possible. But the artificial questions which have arisen because of an inadequate approach to faith are obstacles to understanding.

After suggesting a description of faith, then, I will proceed to explain what it means. Having presented some preliminary explanations in this chapter, I will in those following attempt to put the description into "practice," indicating its implications in terms relating concretely to human experience.

1. A DESCRIPTION

Christian faith is a claim to an accurate understanding of this world, human existence and the gracious Being of God; an understanding which is given in the being, life, actions and teachings of Jesus Christ; and one which calls for and makes possible the humanization of men and the worship of God the Father, in a community witnessing to the presence of his kingdom on earth.

Consider the "direction" of the above description of faith. The Christian in faith looks into the world, not beyond it to a God totally separated from it. It involves an insight into this world and human life in this world, and a claim to perceive a certain significance therein. It is this-worldly, not otherworldly. The only world with which faith deals is this real world.

An example will perhaps clarify the point. Consider the chemist who has been laboring in his laboratory for months, compiling data concerning a problem in the area of fluid mechanics. He has performed hundreds of experiments, measuring heat, friction, viscosity and conduction. He has compiled reams of notes. Day after day he examines and studies the data, seeking to formulate his findings into a significant hypothesis or theory. Suddenly, one afternoon, he examines his data once again. For the first time he notices relationships among the data which he had neglected to note previously. The theory which now emerges is not simply the result of the facts gathered; for the chemist had compiled that data some time before and had carefully examined and re-examined it. The theory is born through the chemist's creative and interpretative insight into the data, not from the addition of further information.

The three important elements in this experience are: (a) the data, obtained by valid experimentation; (b) the significance of the data; which was (c) recognized at a given moment by the chemist. The data itself revealed the basis for the new theory. Yet that theory was not simply lying there as such, the object of the instruments of measurement. It was the result of a creative insight into the data: recognizing, interpreting, formulating a hypothesis.

The emergent theory represents the scientist's claim to an understanding of the meaning of the information, a claim important because it involves an insight into the same information not yet interpreted or made intelligible by other scientists.

Consider another example, similar to that of Geddes Mac-

Gregor in his book, *Introduction to Religious Philosophy*.[1] A baby is born, normally healthy in every way except for one: he is blind. As he matures, he lives in several worlds of perception: he hears sounds, smells odors, senses objects, tastes food. But his world is sightless and colorless. When he is ten years old, he undergoes an operation on his eyes which enables him to see for the first time. The objects of the world in which he had lived for ten years are suddenly present visually to him for the first time. His experience, upon gaining the sense of sight, is that of entering into a world of experience previously inaccessible to him: color.

Let us return to the chemist for a moment. He has experiences of improved perception each time he places a chemical sample under his microscope. The miscroscope allows him to see tiny components in the sample which are invisible to his naked eye. Similarly, the astronomer, when he trains his telescope on a distant star formation for the first time, sees more of what has been there all the time.

Whether the object of perception is the normal world of everyday experience, the microworld of molecules and electron-tracks or the macroworld of galaxies and stars, it is always possible to see more deeply into what is already there, by improving powers of perception.[2] Such improvement can be organic or artificial, that is, by means of scientific equipment. Worlds of experience become accessible and reveal themselves to persons who progressively improve their powers of perception. "Revela-

[1] Cf. Geddes MacGregor, *Introduction to Religious Philosophy* (Boston: Houghton, Mifflin, 1959), pp. 22–28.

[2] Zen Buddhists, such as D. Suzuki, speak of the experience of *satori*, or enlightenment, as central to the religious experience of Zen. Although it is not describable, Suzuki does indicate that one effect of such an experience is that the person participating in it sees more deeply into the world and lives his life in a greater context of meaning. Gautama Buddha himself claimed to be "enlightened" (Buddha), and to have lived the remainder of his years with increased powers of perception. Cf. Suzuki, "Satori," in William Barrett, ed., *Zen Buddhism* (Garden City, N.Y.: Doubleday, 1956), pp. 83–108.

tion" in this context is a matter of looking more deeply into what is there, rather than looking beyond what is there. It is an insight into reality, not a recurring search for superfluous realms of being.

Faith, although it is certainly not identical with chemical investigation or patterns of visibility, involves insight into this world. The Christian claims to recognize a certain meaning, revealed partly by the world and human existence itself.

The second important notion in the explanation of the description of faith is selective perception. In their sense perception of reality, human beings notice a relatively small portion of it. More positively expressed, men utilize a tiny fraction of their awareness-potential, being aware of some things and not of others. Moreover, they select what they perceive according to what they value as most important. Again, some examples should illustrate this observation.

Our friend the chemist finds himself walking down the street one day with his brother, who is a sculptor. They are carrying on a pleasant conversation, and, after talking and walking for fifteen minutes or so, they find a small cafe and stop to have a cup of coffee. There are two factors to notice.

Neither the chemist nor his brother could, if they were asked, tell exactly how many people had passed them as they were walking. Neither is aware of the number of ants he had stepped on, or the number of automobile horns which had blared during the stroll. Nobody is totally aware of all that he encounters. Each person notices and remembers only that to which he pays some attention. We have all had the experience of having a conversation with someone and of being so absorbed in it that other sounds and sights receded from our conscious awareness. There are objects and sounds on the fringes of that awareness. But we recall them only vaguely, or forget them completely afterwards.

Another common experience is that of reading a book or watching television, and hearing another person in the room make an announcement. "Dinner is served." The words sink slowly, over a period of several minutes, into our awareness. We fail to be aware of much of our world because we cannot pay conscious attention to everything. We notice and remember some sounds and sights; we fail to notice, or else forget, many more. We are selective in our perception of reality.[3]

Furthermore, we determine the objects of our conscious and selective perception according to what we think to be important, what we are looking and listening for. The two men in the cafe have recently traveled a few blocks together—in the same city, at the same time, under the same weather conditions. Yet their remembered experiences are different. The chemist may recall the substance of the conversion, the models of some of the cars he passed, some of the outfits adorning the attractive women walking by. His brother, a sculptor, may remember some of the buildings, a spire or a fountain. Each person values certain realities, or aspects of reality, more than others, selecting his experiences according to an inbuilt priority-scale of importance. Each tunes some things in, while tuning the rest out, according to what he deems important.

Our selective perception is conditioned both physiologically and psychologically. In other words, we perceive reality according to the qualities of our senses and according to our educational background and psychological characteristics. During a walk, the sculptor noticed the buildings and the fountains, while his brother did not. We perceive what we come to value as important.

The chemist in his laboratory not only must be able to see and to use his microscope correctly. He also must have an adequate background in chemistry, to allow him to notice what is chemically significant about that which he sees. Moreover, as he experiments in the laboratory, examining the data, he has to be paying conscious attention to as many aspects of the experiment as possible. Even so, he will never be aware of everything which occurs in a given experiment.

[3] Cf. John Cobb, *The Structure of Christian Existence* (Philadelphia: Westminster Press, 1967).

Faith also involves a claim to recognize meaning in this world and in human life, a recognition according to a scale of value-priorities which makes that insight and discovery possible. A doctor experiences an X-ray plate in a manner significantly different from that of his patient. For the latter has no understanding of what to look for, or even where to look. Two persons can observe the same event or object and retain experiences which are qualitatively different. Neither one, moreover, experiences all that is present in any one event or object.

No human being can ever claim total awareness of any aspect of reality. Rather, each selectively perceives and becomes aware of only part of the world which he senses. Improved sense perception or better educational background permit a depth of perception previously or presently inaccessible to everyone. Thus the claim that there is a depth of reality, beyond the normal powers of conscious perception, which nonetheless is really discernible in events and objects of reality, cannot be rejected as meaningless. Who can draw the line? Who can tell us with certainty when we have reached the limits of our powers of perception and our educated understanding of the world? The "mind-expanding" drugs are, if nothing else, an indication that the man who attempts to set *a priori* boundaries to the powers of human perception is being presumptious and unrealistic.

It is not that drugs are the best way for a person to expand and deepen his sense-perception. Regardless for the moment of the means, the fact remains that the limits can be proclaimed only when they have been reached. And they have not been so reached.[4]

2. IN THE OLD TESTAMENT

It is of partial value to read the Old Testament writings, and to reach the conclusion that Revelation is a "process whereby God

[4] Cf. MacGregor, *op. cit.*, pp. 24–27.

reveals himself to men." Such an expression is unfortunate because it limits our selective perception of the meaning of Revelation to God alone. It contributes to the impression that the content of faith, as the acceptance of Revelation, is a clear and accurate knowledge of "who God is." When our understanding of
Revelation is specified in that way, as being God-centered, it contributes to the formation of serious and unnecessary difficulties,
as we saw in the first chapter.

Faith is an understanding of this world, human existence, and
the graciousness of God, which understanding is specified by the
being, life and teachings of Jesus Christ. It consists in the claim
to perceive significance in this world, its events and history. Christians are persons who dedicate themselves, on the basis of their
selective perception of that significance, to renew the face of the
earth, to bring matter and nature to the service of persons—all
because there is a God who is Father. Faith is an insight into this
world and an understanding of its meaning and value, not primarily a looking beyond this world. No expectation of thunder,
lightning and miracles, events confirming belief which come from
another world, are necessary. This should become clear as we
turn now to the Old Testament.

Revelation in the Old Testament refers to the process whereby
the people of God come to an understanding of their world and
their own destiny. They came to recognize their responsibilities
in and for that world by selectively perceiving in nature and in
historical events the presence and purposive activity of a gracious
Lord.

There are four elements which require explanation. Revelation
is (1) personal; (2) discerned in historical events; (3) interpreted
in and for the sake of the community of faith; and (4) imperative
in mood.

(1) Personal. There are two common ways of using the word
"revelation" in everyday language. The first is impersonal, referring to the communication of information. The service station

attendant, for example, reveals to me the route to the state capitol building. Nothing very profound or extraordinary occurs here: a man simply directs me to a local destination.

Revelation is a richer experience when it occurs between friends. When persons reveal themselves to each other, there is more involved than the transmission of information. There are situations in which persons "show their colors," act in such a way as to expose their usual masks and appearances. No matter what a person says about love, it is his treatment of others which reveals his estimation of them. Revelation can occur personally or impersonally, either through verbal information or personal action.

Persons come to understand themselves, to reveal themselves to themselves. They do so by becoming aware of the ways in which others react to them. If most people who are acquainted with me, for example, describe me as a selfish person, I learn about myself. I necessarily reflect on the ways in which I have conducted myself in order to create that reaction in others.

There are situations in which persons reveal themselves importantly to themselves, as well as to others. The man who, in an emergency, instinctively puts the safety of others before his own, understands himself better after the experience than he did before. There are certain events and situations in which persons reveal themselves, both to others and to themselves, in an accurate way.

The Old Testament people learned as much about themselves as they did about God. They claimed that they had undergone certain experiences, participated in certain events, which had in an unusual but profound manner revealed to them their meaning or purpose, both as a people and as individuals. This purpose included the responsibility of making a world according to God's will. The revelation involved is not primarily informational. It is understood most accurately in a personal context.

(2) Discerned in historical events. There are two important

factors here. First, Revelation in the Old Testament involved a process of looking into historical events, instead of awaiting miraculous, extrahistorical manifestations of God. The fact that the God of Israel revealed the meaning of human life in the world through historical events, moreover, and not through the cycles of nature, committed the people to understand their responsibility to participate in historical events, not to look beyond this world to another.

More succinctly, what was revealed was their understanding of themselves and of their role in the world, a world in the process of being created by their God. Their primary responsibility was in and for this world: they were "stewards" of God's creation. This understanding found symbolic expression in their liturgy in which they celebrated events, not theories. Their origin and their destiny were this-worldly; widespread expectations of extrahistorical salvation were not prevalent until the time of the Babylonian Exile, about 580 B.C. That is a period of over seven hundred years after the time of the Exodus, and over twelve hundred years after the formation of the first covenant with the patriarch Abraham. They were tied in their origins as a people, their growing understanding of the graciousness of God, and their destiny, to this world.

This leads to an important observation. In its creation and vocation to become a garden in which all nature and mankind would live in harmony (described in the account of Adam and Eve in Eden), this world, its matter and its history, provided the locus and content of Revelation and faith. The claim to Revelation was a claim that this world, its matter, its animals and its persons were intrinsically linked in significance and in goals. God's Revelation is not about heaven or about the world of the supernatural. He was saying that this world has meaning because it is a cosmos: an ordered world, manifesting the presence of its creator, and becoming increasingly the locus of his relationship with his people. Historical events, then, became the key to the understanding by the Old Testament people of this world. This is a world which has meaning and value in terms of its existence under the stewardship of men. And men in turn are meant to transform it in fundamental harmony.

(3) This brings us to the third element in our description of Old Testament Revelation: its involving an interpretation of this world and of historical events by prophetic individuals.

Recall the discussion above in which we pointed to certain events which provided opportunities for distinctly personal revelations by individuals. These events occur when the "chips are down." Our knowledge of any person depends importantly upon, and results from, certain key events in which that person expresses himself most profoundly. Upon hearing that a friend has been accused of embezzling funds from the establishment at which he is employed, I exclaim, "Melvin would never do such a thing." The basis for that statement is my knowledge of and confidence in Melvin, which have been formed during those occasions on which Melvin demonstrated to me his basic and consistent honesty.

So also, it is possible to discover in the Old Testament events which are decisive, which remain in the recollection of the people as effectively determining their knowledge of the world, of themselves and of their God. The most significant of those events was the one which most clearly manifested the Being-of-God-for-them. It revealed, simultaneously, the meaning and responsibility of their existence, socially and individually, in this world. This was the event of Exodus.

It was in the Exodus event that the covenant emerged as the bond among Israelites, and between them and their God, Yahweh. The covenant, reaccepted in each Passover celebration by succeeding generations, revealed the loving Being-of-God-for-them. It revealed, simultaneously, their obligation to accept the task of building a community of faith in the world. Each Passover was a celebration of the event of Exodus, which remained as the basis for Israel's claim to Revelation and provided the perduring value-scale by which the prophets interpreted succeeding historical events.

The prophet in Israel was the religiously sensitive and perceptive man who, as a member of the covenant people, perceived the significance in key historical events selectively, according to the covenantal value-scale. Revelation continued as prophets improved the ability of the Israelite people to understand their world, their own existence and their God, by looking more deeply into historical events and understanding their significance.

It is always necessary to interpret historical events. No historian, obviously, is merely a chronicler of names, dates, and places. The competent historian of the American Civil War, for example, is able to relate a multiplicity and complexity of personages and occurrences in terms of causes and effects. He looks "below the surface," as it were, recognizing the meaning of certain battle victories, defeats, political intrigues, et cetera. There is an adage to the effect that hindsight is more accurate than present observation. The historian is able to interpret the significance of battles, presidential elections or assassinations more accurately if some years intervene to allow for further compilation of facts and for more reflection.

Lastly, every historian of repute examines his data with certain presuppositions and interests, selectively perceiving the data and composing his narratives. There are military historians, as well as historians whose specialization is intellectual, cultural, economic or political history. History is a selectively perceived and interpreted account of the past, written from a perspective which allows for the recognition of significance not clearly evident to contemporaries of the period under analysis.

The Old Testament is an historical account of the process by which a people came to an understanding of themselves, their world and their responsibilities for it. This understanding evolved through the creative insights of certain prophetic individuals, who selectively interpreted historical events according to the value-scale provided by the covenant. Faith demanded of the Israelites not that they articulate their belief in the existence of the sky-God Yahweh. They were faithful insofar as they participated in the history of the chosen people, exercising stewardship in the world by accepting responsibility for it.

Significant events can have a number of possible meanings; they must be interpreted. For example, if a large friend of mine, upon encountering me one afternoon, slaps me vigorously on the back, I will be very interested in the words which interpret the meaning of the action. The action itself comprises only one part of the whole event. The event can only be interpreted accurately when my friend speaks. If he says, "Hello, old friend!" then his gesture is one of friendship. If, on the other hand, his words are, "I resent what you said about my wife," then the whole episode becomes an unpleasant one. Understanding the meaning of the slap, I will attempt to extricate myself from the situation.

Events as such demand interpretation in order to be accurately understood. In the Old Testament, historical events were the medium of Revelation because of the presence in the community of Israel of prophets who interpreted them, specified the meaning of a given event among the various possible meanings. The criterion which continued to provide the priority-scale of interpretation in Israel was the covenant formed in the Exodus event.

The people of Israel, in the sixth century B.C., found themselves led away into exile in Babylonia. This was not merely a result of military defeat. In terms of the prophetic interpretations of Jeremiah and Deutero-Isaiah, the people understood these events as signifying their own infidelity to their covenant with Yahweh.

Biblical Revelation therefore included both objective and subjective components. The historical events took place, constituting objective reference points. But they awaited interpretation by individuals able to perceive, according to their understanding of the people and their traditions in the light of the covenant, the significance of those events.

That prophetic interpretation took cultic and ritualistic expression in liturgical celebrations commemorating the most important of the revelatory events, the Exodus from Egypt. As sacred history proceeded, constituted by events and their prophetic interpretations, various groups undertook the task of recording these sacred events for the sake of generations to come. Scripture took its origin from the liturgical celebrations of the people of God, celebrations symbolically interpreting the events which they had witnessed and experienced. The Bible, then, is not a source of Revelation, but a witness to it. It is a product of the community which partially articulated its understanding of its world, its own meaning and value, and its God.

(4) The mood is imperative. Faith, then, does not refer to the reception of certain information about God. Its context is personal; it is an insight into the world through historical events. Because one component of that insight is the awareness of a God who loves men, there could be no indifference to the understanding. To acknowledge Revelation in faith in this personal context is not simply to make an intellectual judgment as to its veracity. It is to accept a concomitant responsibility.

We find ourselves sometimes relatively indifferent to the existence of most people. We can acknowledge the existence of so many people we casually encounter without acknowledging an obligation toward them, except for that of respecting their dignity as persons. This is not to say that other people make no difference to us; but only that the fact of the existence of most of them does not demand from us any response except the attempt to accord them respect.

But there are other persons whose existence causes us to determine our lives in particular ways. For they have revealed more than the matter of fact that they exist. These persons are of two "categories": personal friends and influential personalities.

Once we know that another person really wishes to give of himself or herself to us, to be at our service in a way which constitutes a risk to his or her well-being, the situation changes. Revelation is personal. Our acknowledgment of that person's existence is at the same time either an acceptance of the friendship or love involved or a rejection of it. We cannot remain indifferent. Our attempt to do so would in itself be a willful rejection of the person. For we recognize not simply the existence of that person, but the existence of that person for us.[5]

Perhaps political assasinations illustrate how persons can have a profound effect on one another, despite never having actually met. Although he did not know Dr. Martin Luther King personally, for the assassin in Memphis, Tennessee, Dr. King's existence was no matter of indifference. The very being of Dr. King in a racist American society was a challenge and a threat to many persons. The response of one of them was to shoot and to kill, thereby seeking to eliminate the threat embodied by Martin Luther King. For to acknowledge the very existence of the man was to accept or to reject the principles which informed that existence and gave it substance: principles of equality and dignity for persons of every race.

Each day Christians gather to commemorate the assassination of Jesus of Nazareth. That assassination was an attempt by some individuals to eliminate the threat to their lives symbolized by Jesus. That event, celebrated daily, is the occasion for millions of persons to accept the demands made by Christ, to attempt to structure their own lives accordingly.

As Fr. Murray has noted, the atheist in Israel was not just the man who had made the erroneous intellectual judgment that God does not exist.[6] The acknowledgment of God's being included the acceptance of his being-for-men, and created the obligation to accept or reject the corresponding demand to live accordingly. Rejecting Revelation was therefore a matter of refus-

[5] Cf. David Jenkins, *The Glory of Man* (New York: Scribner's, 1967), pp. 1–24.

[6] Cf. Murray, *The Problem of God* (New Haven: Yale University Press, 1964), part 1.

ing not only to admit the existence of God, or to recognize his gracious being. It was also a refusal to accept responsibility in the world.

In the Old Testament, Revelation consisted in the process whereby the people of God developed their understanding, not only of God, but of this world, and their significance and responsibilities in and for this world. They developed these insights by selectively perceiving, through the instrumentality of the prophetic interpretative words, the significance of historical events. This recognition gave them social and personal identity, and remained to make up the value-scale by which to interpret succeeding events. Faith was not God-centered. That is, it was not just the belief in God, based upon a desire to understand his nature. It rather comprised a claim to recognize meaning in this world, as well as the obligation to make that meaning known to other men.

3. IN THE NEW TESTAMENT

With this background it is possible to explain more fully the meaning of the statements, "Jesus Christ is the Revelatory Event of God"; "God was in Jesus Christ, reconciling the world to himself"; and "God is Love." The Christian's faith is totally specified by the being, life, teachings and actions of Jesus Christ, the fullness of Revelation.

As we have indicated, the claim by the Christian to accept Revelation is specified totally by his acceptance of Jesus as Lord. That means that the Christian makes no claim to know God as he exists in himself. Rather, he claims to recognize the meaning and value of his world and human existence because of the Revelation of Jesus Christ. He claims to recognize God insofar as he has acted in the events comprising the being, life, teachings and actions of Christ. To accept Christian Revelation in faith is to accept a vision of the world, of human life and of God-for-men-in-Christ.[7]

Christ is the retroactive Revelation of the world, human life and the graciousness of God. Thus he is, as St. John and generations of Christians have asserted, the *Word* of God. An example should clarify the meaning of the phrase "retroactive revelation."

As I begin to compose this sentence, I string words together in a certain way. As I do so, the meaning of the sentence as a whole begins to become clearer—until the sentence ends, and the meaning is finally clear. Notice that the last word in the sentence, "Arnold is——" is of decisive importance. It is the last word which retroactively gives full significance to the first words: a significance which could not become clear until the sentence is finished.

Christ is the last Word of God. In his existence, life and actions and teachings are the key and decisive events, with their interpretations by the Word, which constitute for the Christian his understanding of reality. Because the most decisive Revelatory Event for the Christian is the series of events comprising the Event of Jesus Christ, it reveals retroactively the significance of the prior key events in sacred history, such as the Exodus. It also reveals the meaning of human history as such, as well as the meaning of the process of evolution. More will be said about this in the third chapter.

How can a series of events be called an "Event?" It is common to refer to the War of 1812 as an "important event in American history." Everyone is aware that this "event" actually denotes thousands, even millions, of discreet occurrences and experiences which took place during those months, both in England and in North America. The War of 1812 is a significant historical Event comprising millions of separate events related historically in terms of their association with the war. Each individual event must be considered in its relationship to the other events to be intelligible.

7 Cf. Jenkins, *op. cit.*, ch. 2.

The Christian asserts with St. Matthew that Christ is the fulfillment of the Old Testament Revelation. Those events recorded in the Old Testament now can be understood as pointing in their effective significance to the Incarnation. For the Christian the statement "God acts in history" is anchored in the historical Event of Jesus of Nazareth.

Christ determines the Christian's understanding of Revelation. To consider the meaning of the phrase "Revelation of Christ," let us utilize the same categories as those we used in discussing Revelation in the Old Testament.

(1) Personal. The understanding which Christ communicates, as was the case in the Old Testament, is not simply or completely the information that there is a God. Although in the Gospels he does refer to his Father frequently, and spends long hours in prayer, urging those who would follow him to do the same, he delivers no lectures on the nature of God. Christ's teaching is composed of claims about what this world is like. This is the content of Revelation: that this world is a certain kind of world, because it is under the rule of God. Because this world is, as a matter of fact, one in which brotherhood is meant to obtain among men, loving one's neighbor is much more effective in attaining that goal than killing him or stealing from him.

This is an essential point. Christ is speaking about a fact: that this world has significance and value in terms of human persons. Thus love, not hypocrisy, dishonesty or hatred, is the effective agent in realizing that value. Men are brothers.

Furthermore, as was the case for the Old Testament people, Revelation for Christians comprises the definitive understanding, in and through Christ, of the gracious Being of God for men and the possibilities for human freedom. This is one insight into the phrase of Father Edward Schillebeeckx, when he refers to Christ as the "Sacrament of the encounter with God": that the individual, Jesus Christ, speaks the final and most profound divine word concerning what it means to be human.

This elucidates partially the meaning of St. Augustine's dictum,

"Facta Verbi verba": the deeds of the Word are words themselves. Christ's actions and specifying words provide the true understanding of the world, human existence and the Father's love for men. St. John in his Gospel designates the miracles of Christ as "signs," whereby Jesus revealed his glory. The miracles—indeed, all the events constituting the Event of Christ—must be understood in this way. Christ's multiplication of the loaves and the fishes, recorded in Matthew's Gospel, is not a "trick" to demonstrate his divinity. It is an action which speaks Christ as the source of life.

(2) This brings us to the second element in our analysis: historical events. Certain historical events in the Old Testament were seen as key and revelatory, providing the criteria for understanding the nature of reality. They made up the means by which the people of God acquired their insight into reality and progressively perfected their understanding of that reality. The Incarnation is for Christians *the* key historical event which, because it initiates the Christ-Event, opens up the possibility for accurately understanding historical existence itself. The actions and words of Jesus interpret his own Incarnation as the central Revelatory historical Event of God.

The real meaning of the Incarnation, moreover, becomes clearer as human history moves toward Parousia, the second coming of Christ. It is only in our own day, for instance, that the command of Christ to "go and teach all nations" is becoming intelligible. For those who first heard those words were extremely restricted in their knowledge of the dimensions of the planet, the persons living on every continent, et cetera. In other words, the mandate really only becomes meaningful when, in our own day, its physical presuppositions are present: the communications network which is slowly creating a world community. Before persons can love one another, they must know one another. Improved transportation and communications facilities are making this possible.

The fact that historical development is necessary in order that the intelligibility of the Christ-Event become progressively manifest points up the necessity for a perduring community of persons who are able to provide effective and accurate interpretations of the demands of the Gospel, as well as indicating the pertinence of that Gospel to the events of ongoing human history. The scientist who devotes his life to the construction and implementation of the lines of world communication, then, is participating directly in the process of making Revelation present and effective in men's lives.

The New Testament is a collection of writings which recorded and interpreted the Revelatory events which had recently occurred. As in the Old Testament, these writings arose from early Christian liturgical celebrations, celebrations of the Revelatory Event of Christ. Again, Revelation is not to be understood as a set of theses or propositions. It refers to a vision of this world, human existence and God, which occurred in Jesus Christ, the fulfillment of the covenant-promise made in the Old Testament.

This is the reason why the New Testament writings are normative for succeeding Christians' experience of faith. They bear witness to the Revelatory Event of Christ which commenced with the fact of his Incarnation. Like the Exodus event in the Old Testament, the Event of Christ finds expression in regular liturgical celebration, remaining as the key Event by which Christians understand this world, the meaning of human existence and the gracious Being of God.

(4) The mood of Christian Revelation is imperative, not merely indicative. The Crucifixion occurred partly because Christ's existence threatened certain individuals. Some, choosing to remain in the darkness, rejected the light. The Crucifixion, as a saving event in the process of Christian Revelation, reveals both the love of God for men and the strange, frightening depth of evil present within human life. For in crucifying Jesus, men revealed themselves to be terrified by the demands of love which this man made upon them.

When theology speaks of the Crucifixion as taking place under the power of sin, it means that it was an event in which the powers of human beings to perpetuate evil, and consequently, their need for redemption, were revealed in the same event. It is this event by which Christ demonstrated the more effective power of grace, the love of God for men.

Ours is an age in which the theological emphasis has been placed upon the Resurrection of Christ as the central mystery of faith. It is important, however, that Christians remain conscious of the revelation of the depth of evil present in human life manifested in the Crucifixion. Certainly that power is evident. Insight into the meaning of the Crucifixion must, for the Christian, show up as superficial the humanist's blind confidence that economic prosperity or education will eradicate evil from the world.

The continuing celebrations of the Christ-Event each day since his immolation provide opportunities for every human generation not only to understand themselves and their world, but to accept responsibility for that world. To acknowledge the historical existence of Alexander the Great demands no profound response on my part. To accept the Revelatory Event of Jesus Christ is at the same time to accept his demands upon me, to take a stand about the nature of human existence itself.[8] Christ is the Revelation of God and of man. The Christ-Event communicates the accurate understanding of this world, human life and God-for-men. Revelation involves this world, and its acceptance by a man demands a different way of life, a conversion. "God acts in history" means that God has acted, and continues to act, in the historical Event of Jesus of Nazareth, the Christ.

Just as the Incarnation is the event which retroactively reveals the meaning of the Revelatory events preceding it in the history of the people of God, so the Resurrection of Christ is the central and most important Revelatory event in history for Christians. That event reveals retroactively the full significance of the Incarnation of Christ, his public life, his words, his actions and his

8 *Ibid.*, ch. 4.

death. It is the most articulate divine Revelatory word spoken, and constitutes the most that God the Father can say to men: sons. It makes possible the most significant word in response possible for men: Abba, Father.

As Fr. Peter DeRosa has explained, the Resurrection cannot be treated apologetically as a "proof" for Christ's divinity.[9] Rather, it is the basis for Christian faith, providing the value-scale for the interpretation of this world, human life and God's love for men. That Christ has risen bodily is the definitive sign of God's fidelity to his covenant. The risen Christ lives bodily. That completes the process whereby the matter of this world realizes its potential to be totally at the service of human persons and of God. That the Resurrection is an event involved with human history recommits the Christian community to service in and of this world. It's mission is to "build the earth," in the words of Fr. Pierre Teilhard de Chardin. The Incarnation, Crucifixion and Resurrection of Christ, the Christ-Event, imply that "material" concerns, "corporal works of mercy," do not take second position on the priority-scale of Christian values. Service of persons is service of bodily persons. The existence of Christ is fundamentally linked to that of this world. Christian faith is this worldly.

Similarly, the meaning and value of human life is revealed in the Resurrection. Christians understand human existence in terms of the kenosis, Christ's self-emptying act of love for men on Calvary and in Resurrection. The Resurrection makes possible for him who accepts it "response-ability": the ability, because death is not the annihilation of persons, to respond to others because those others will never cease to be. Accepting this understanding of human existence in general is to accept responsibility particularly for one's influence upon the lives of others.

The Resurrection is the Revelatory Event of God. "God loves his people," for the Christian, is a statement with definite empiri-

9 Cf. Peter DeRosa, *Christ and Original Sin* (Milwaukee: Bruce, 1967).

cal and historical content. It is not an airy abstraction, but a statement of fact based upon the death of Jesus Christ and the empty tomb on Easter morning. St. John said, "God is Love." The meaning of that statement is clear to the Christian who reads the account of the Christ-Event in Scripture as a member of the community of faith. "Greater love than this hath no man": Christ's life specifies the meaning of this statement.

Now when we describe Christian faith as the acceptance of the Revelation of Christ, that description is meaningful. Faith, to repeat our earlier description, is a claim to an accurate understanding of human existence, this world and the gracious Being of God; an understanding which is given in the be-ing (Event), life, actions and teachings of Jesus Christ; and one which calls for and makes possible the humanization of men and the worship of God the Father in a community witnessing to the presence of his kingdom on earth. Faith is a claim to knowledge of this world, not of the essence or existence of a supernaturally distant God. Faith develops within the Christian community, expressed by persons in liturgical celebrations and in their lives insofar as they are informed by its priority-scale of values.

4. EXISTENTIAL INTERPRETATIONS

At this point it is necessary to indicate a danger implicit in describing faith as an insight into this world: that one's interpretation of the meaning of "objective" events is by nature partial and subjective. The question is, whose interpretation is correct? Different people see different meanings in the same event. What provides the norm for accurate interpretation?

We have attempted to "objectify" the faith-understanding of Christians by pointing to the existence of a value-scale, fully present only in the Christ-Event. But experience immediately reminds us that people can, within limits, "use" Christ to justify any conceivable interpretation. He has, in fact, been the professed motive for the Crusades, as well as for the slaughter of witches in New England and the outlawing of evolutionist biologists in Arkansas and Tennessee classrooms.

Within the discipline of theology, the "existentialist" school of biblical interpretation, under the leadership of Rudolf Bultmann, has influenced both contemporary Protestant and Catholic thought. Inspired by the widening disparity between the growing body of scientific knowledge and the literalist understanding by so many Christians of Scriptural passages, Bultmann's principal purpose was to translate the message of Christian faith into terminology meaningful and powerful for contemporary man.[10] He was also convinced that the ontology of Martin Heidegger, developed in *Being and Time,* provided the key to the meaningful contemporary translation of the Gospel which he sought.

Bultmann, in attempting to "demythologize" the New Testament writings, tended to treat them as documents providing for contemporary man a way of understanding his own existence, as an opportunity to make an ultimate decision about that existence. He called attention to the mythological framework of the Gospels. As documents produced by human minds and hands shortly after the death of Jesus in Palestine during the first century, they must be considered in their historical context. It is therefore necessary to attempt to understand the ways in which the authors of the Bible considered the world. It is necessary to discover and investigate the meaning of the cosmological and religious presuppositions commonly accepted by the community in which these writings arose.

For example, the early Christians, sharing the beliefs of human beings in the area at the time, envisioned reality in a trilayered manner, consisting of a world of the "beyond," this world, and an underworld inhabited by dark and mysterious spirits. Consequently, in order to understand passages dealing with

10 Cf. Rudolf Bultmann, *Jesus Christ and Mythology* (New York: Scribner's, 1958), for a fuller and more adequate treatment.

"angels" and "devils" in the New Testament writings, one must interpret them, not accept them as evidence that such beings actually exist. Angels and devils were the spiritual "furniture" of the way men looked at reality, much as men today simply presuppose that the earth is elliptical, existing as one planet among others. There was as little reason to think otherwise at that time about angels and devils as there is today regarding the planetary situation of the earth.

Thus the existentialist interpreter would discourage the belief in actual, objective divine interventions into the created order of things. Accepting such interventions would be most difficult for modern "scientific" man. The Gospel writings should be interpreted, not as actually descriptive of events, but as statements about human existence intended to provide the occasions for contemporary moments of choice for men. Miracles would be examples of such divine interventions, important only insofar as they give an understanding of human existence.

Because men today no longer think in terms of a three-layered world, or even a two-layered natural-supernatural) cosmos, they cannot be asked to believe in a mythological message until it has been "demythologized," stripped of its attachment to the mythic presuppositions of a bygone age. Men today simply do not find it easy to accept the Christian belief that Jesus arose bodily from the grave. Consequently, the Resurrection must not be presented to men by Christians as a real event, miraculous and true. It is important only insofar as it articulates truths about human existence, such as that life can emerge from death. The only understanding, really, which the Christian tradition can give is an understanding of human existence. There is no claim to a real knowledge of God.

Without attempting to be complete in this analysis, it is sufficient to indicate, with Father Leopold Malevez, some of the inadequacies in such an approach.[11] On first glance, it may seem

---

[11] Cf. Leopold Malevez, *The Christian Message and Myth: The Theology of Rudolf Bultmann*, trans. O. Wyon (Westminster, Md.: Newman Press, 1958).

that the analysis of Revelation and faith presented in the first section of this chapter is an existential one, for it seeks to locate Christian faith in this world, speaking about human existence in the world.

But the "existential" analysis criticized by Malevez and others allows no possibility for the recognition of what is basic and central in Christian faith: the experience of grace, or sharing in the life of God-in-Christ. Christ's status, in fact, becomes hopelessly ambiguous. One may also note that for men of two thousand years ago it was just as difficult as it is for men of today to understand how a man dead and buried could rise to life.

The purpose of this short reference to the existentialist school has been to call attention to the dangers present in emphasizing the this-worldliness of Christian faith to such an extent that any kind of criterion for assessing the accuracy or inaccuracy of that faith is lost. If the truth resides only in a person's subjective encounter and involvement with it, then the truth of Christian faith becomes but an extension of subjective needs, desires or demands.

During the remainder of this book the reader should bear in mind this danger. It will be my contention that there are, of necessity, criteria for assessing the accuracy of the Christian's claim to faith, criteria present both within his own tradition and outside it, that is, in human experience.

Selective perception and interpretation are involved in the vision of faith, a vision oriented toward this world. Realizing that the being or Event of Christ specifies the scale of values present in that interpretation objectifies the matter somewhat. But as we have noticed, because persons have occasionally used Christ to justify various courses of action, there must be some further norm of interpretation.

All Christian traditions have acknowledged the necessary function of the New Testament writings. Because these writings originated in the experiential witness of men who lived with

Jesus for three years, they remain normative for the experience of faith by Christians for all time. If the experience which later Christians have of Christ is of a Christ other than the one presented in the Gospels, it is inauthentic.

But Christian history reveals the appearance, with the passage of time and the encounter by the Christian community of men of different cultures, of questions not susceptible to answers in the categories of the New Testament as such. "Who is Christ?" is an example. The answer, "He is the Messiah," makes much sense to a Jew. But to a person belonging to a tradition which is not Jewish, which does not possess a word or concept equivalent to "messiah," the answer does not suffice. There arises the necessity, therefore, within the Christian community to reflect upon and translate the message of the Gospel into the language and thought-patterns of men in different cultures. This process is known as theology.

After a short discussion of some of the functions of theology, then, we will attempt to understand why, in the light of a necessary norm for the accuracy of faith, for theological interpretation and application of that norm to men in every age, there must be a teaching authority of some kind within the Christian community. We will attempt, in other words, to explain why we included, in the description of Christian faith at the beginning of this chapter, the phrase, ". . . makes possible the humanization of men and the worship of God the Father *in a community* witnessing to the presence of his kingdom on earth."

5. THEOLOGY, FAITH, REVELATION

Theology is the intellectual reflection upon, and articulation of, aspects of the experience of Christian faith. By means of theology the community maintains and deepens its understanding of Revelation, thereby enriching its experience of faith. Theology is *fides quaerens intellectum,* in the words of St. Anselm: faith seeking understanding. It is an activity within the Christian community which arises from the experience of faith, and it serves to enrich that experience by making the content of faith more accurately accessible to the mind.

As in the preceding section, it is possible to explain the above description by isolating some elements. Theology is: (1) the reflection upon, and partial conceptual expression of, Christian faith; (2) by individuals within the community of faith; (3) which reflection and partial articulation contributes to the evolution by the community as a whole of its understanding both of Revelation and of those elements in a given human culture which are compatible with Christian faith; and (4) which is caused by factors both internal and external.

Theology is the reflection upon, and articulation of, aspects of the experience of faith. There are two presuppositions here: (a) that concepts are a valid and necessary means of communicating experiences; but that (b) their value is but partial, insofar as they are successful in that communication.

Contrary to the "demythologizers" who assert that this age is one in which men have moved away from myths, Dr. Herbert Richardson reminds us that this is an age which reflects myths of its own.[12] The Nazi myth of the superrace was instrumental only a few years ago in the rise to ascendancy and development of a threat to world security by Adolf Hitler in Germany. It spawned themes and theme songs, created instant emotional responses by millions of Germans to the demands of the dictator. The contemporary American hippie phenomenon is at least an indication of a rejection of the "Horatio Alger" myth underlying the American capitalistic value-scale, which exalts economic self-sufficiency as the highest human ideal. Myths are not absent; they are simply different, or capable of being differentiated.

Because the language of myth is symbolic, it takes the form of

12 On the modern capacity to differentiate myths, cf. H. Richardson, *Towards an American Theology* (New York: Macmillan, 1967).

words susceptible to various meanings, which elicit emotional responses from persons in the process of cummunicating a degree of intellectual understanding. There has arisen in our own day a real distrust of the concept, whose only value is that it represents an idea accurately for the sake of communication. This anticonceptualism manifests itself in the American Catholic Church, especially among the youth, in the current distaste for dogmas and *Baltimore Catechism No. 2*, which stand for an approach to religion which is arid, abstract and bloodless. Certainly one significant factor in the decisions by universities to reduce the number of theology courses which students are required to take is the reaction by students to courses in theology which are dry.

I concur in the decision by Catholic universities to reduce the number of required theology courses. However, insofar as the current antirationalism suggests or implies that, because certain doctrines and solemn Church teachings are abstract, they are unnecessary to any individual Christian's experience of faith, I cannot agree.

Concepts and propositions are valid and necessary modes of communicating experiences. Certainly language as such did not appear until human societies began to form. But there is a reciprocity here: historically, societies form languages for the purpose of communication by their constituent members. Conversely, languages make possible and contribute to the well-being and evolution of societies by establishing the possibilities for such communication.

This is true in the lives of individual persons as well. Human beings, in fact, do not become persons until they begin to establish networks of communication with others. The small child requires a language to learn in order to begin communicating with his parents, brothers and sisters. The most prevalent forms of language are obviously the written and spoken words—although in a wider sense language includes gestures and touch sensations and even silence. The point still stands: there is need for an abstract set of signs, one step removed from actual experience, if human communication is to occur. Words are a high form of language because they are abstract symbols. As such, they can point to the greatest possible number of things, and can allow for the participation by all persons who understand their meaning. Touch sensations are limited to particular objects and restricted numbers of participants.

Human life as such would be impossible without language. For the child even to begin thinking, exercising that function of individual personal life which differentiates him from lower forms of animal life, he must utilize language. No person can think without words, spoken silently to himself. Words are necessary as well for those who apparently "think" in images, if communication is to occur. Language is a necessary prerequisite for human life to be human, considered either socially or individually. Although this requirement does not demand any particular language, such as German or French, there is a need for language as such.

However, nobody can totally conceptualize even one experience or series of experiences. The lover rebels at the attempt to analyze his love. For analysis kills love. This holds true whether the analysis originates in his lover or in another. Similarly, the believer who attempts to conceptualize that series of experiences which he designates "religious," will consistently be frustrated. Language limits personal expression as it makes such expression possible. It is a tool for the communication of aspects of experience. Yet it is not the experience; it is one step removed, so to speak. It is abstract.

It is true that words and concepts often interpose between persons, and between persons and their world. To see a tree, and to have that experience largely conditioned by the concept "tree," is to make impossible the intuitive experience of unity which is described in, for example, the parables of Zen Buddhism. Persons use concepts to predetermine their experiences of each other and their world. And faith is one such concept.

But in the public sphere, where human beings must deal with one another socially, economically and politically, concepts are useful. One person can never totally communicate a personal experience to another. But his words, as reflective articulations of aspects of that experience, can at least partially perform the task. Language is a means whereby human beings build a shared world of experience, and fuse together their horizons.

It is possible to speak of a sense in which the community of Christian faith as a whole, through its theologians, reflects upon and articulates aspects of its corporate experience of faith and its continuing understanding of Revelation. Here is a valuable insight into the service which theology performs for the faith of Christians. The magisterium has in fact sanctioned certain theological propositions as partially expressive of the faith of the community.

The basic reason, then, for the existence of theology—and, indirectly, for that of dogmas—lies in the fact that human beings have minds, and that they seek to understand and to express in language more of what they experience. Theology is that activity by certain persons in the community by which they reflect upon and conceptualize aspects of the experience of Christian faith. One of theology's functions, moreover, is to demonstrate the internal intellectual consistency of Christian faith to Christians.

Who is Jesus of Nazareth? What does the personal acceptance in faith of Jesus mean and imply in a given era and cultural situation? These are questions which demand answers, some of which are not given explicitly, in those terms, in Scripture. Theology is that activity by which Christians seek to answer those questions. It is the activity by which the Church as a community reflects upon and conceptualizes throughout history its answers to such questions.[13]

As Father Murray has so clearly described, the early Christian

13 Cf. John H. Cardinal Newman, *An Essay on the Development of Christian Doctrine* (London: Longmans, Green and Co., 1920), ch. 1.

community was faced with a real difficulty as it moved from Palestine into Greece, Rome and the Western world: how to speak of a Jew, Christ Jesus, in Greek terminology.[14] The questions which Greeks asked about Christ demanded answers in concepts not given as such in Scripture. These questions were "external" stimuli, prompting the community to reflect upon and develop its understanding of the experience of faith. Added to the "internal" stimulus, the propensity on the part of reflective Christians to reflect upon faith, it provided impetus to the development of theology. Theology developed as the intellectual confrontation by Christians of questions about Christ and his Father—questions whose answers were not clearly and formally present in the New Testament writings.

Dogmas came into being when, periodically, at the great councils of the early Church, bishops formally rejected as inaccurate certain theological propositions which conflicted with the accurate understanding of Revelation. The heretic, paradoxically, was therefore a significant contributor to the formation of official magisterial teaching. It was he who made the claim to which the magisterium had to respond.

For example, it was the teaching of Arius in the fourth-century Alexandrian community in Egypt which, by implying that Jesus was inferior in status to God the Father, occasioned the convocation of the Council of Nicaea by the Emperor Constantine in 325 A.D. From that council emerged the core of the creed: Jesus Christ is of one substance with the Father.

Theology has in fact served the Christian community consistently since the origins of that community. It has been the methodological tool by which individual Christians have implemented their inherent desire to understand Revelation, and by which the magisterium has responded to heretical challenges to that understanding. It is partial, intellectual, rational, abstract and occasional—providing one means by which the Revelation

14 Cf. Murray, *op. cit.*, part 3.

of Christ confronts thinking human beings. Within the Church it has thus created the theoretical foundations and principles for constant renewal and reformulation. By attempting to present the intellectual aspects and foundations for Christian faith to non-Christians historically, who direct serious questions to the Church of Christ, theology has been the means by which Christians have understood their relevance to the world.

Theology has always been an occasional activity. For, as the reflective articulation of Christian faith caused by the internal necessity for men to understand and express their experience, it is not a constant activity. This is true for the individual Christian, as it is for the Church as a whole.

Not all Christians are theologians. Most believe in God, Jesus Christ, the Holy Spirit, the importance of the Church and post-mortem happiness. They also profess love to be the important standard of human action. Depending upon their education and interests, some Christians step back from their beliefs occasionally, reflect, ask questions and seek answers to those questions. For them theology, present either in periodicals, books or sessions with parish priests, is of periodic value in aiding them to ascertain the intellectual coherence of their faith. Theology's service to persons is occasional.

History reveals a similar characteristic of theological activity in the Church itself. The solemn magisterial moments during which dogmas are born are relatively infrequent. Although these dogmas arise from the constant presence of theological activity within the community, there are periods in history when that activity is more intense than it is at others. There are always present in the community a small percentage of the membership who devote themselves to the task of becoming professional theologians: still, there have been historical periods during which theology's service to the Church at large has been greater than usual.

For example, during the years immediately preceding and following the great councils of the Church, one perceives a more intense level of theological activity because of the presence of serious intellectual challenges to faith. An exceptional period may be our own, in which there is a very intense degree of theological activity without its having been occasioned by specific heretical positions. Of course, such a judgment may be premature.

Theology thus makes possible both the pastoral and apostolic activities of the Church, activities by which the Church continually renews itself and provides for the perpetual opportunities for Christians to understand their faith better. Theology's nature, as contrasted with that of faith, is intellectual and reflective, expressing itself in concepts and propositions once removed from actual experience. Faith, as the acceptance of Christ, the Revelatory Event, involves both an insight or claim to understanding and the acceptance of the demand to change one's mode of living. Christians live out their faith, symbolizing it in prayer and sacrament. Theology arises within the community of faith as a service designed to keep the understanding of faith accurate, to demonstrate the relationship between Christian Revelation and the contemporary world. Theology, as the reflective stepping-back from the experience of faith, is not as rich as that experience itself. It is an occasional activity, whose value should not be overestimated.

But theology is important. Its nature is intellectual and theoretical, in some ways resembling the relationship between theoretical physics and practical or applied physics (engineering). In both cases the theories are the abstract possibilities for practically implementing the principles, solving problems which improve human life as such. Obviously, each can become too abstract. But a viable and healthy theology is indispensable to the Christian community.

Because faith is a claim about this world and human existence as such, theologians in a given historical period have a twofold obligation. They have the responsibility, first, to reflect a loyalty to their fellow Christians by continually suggesting effective steps for renewal and for developing the understanding of what it means to be Christian. They fulfill this responsibility when they succeed in applying valuable insights to the renewal of important aspects of Christian life, when they conduct adult education classes, involve themselves in catechetical work, et cetera.

Secondly, the theologian must be a man of his day. He must discuss the value of faith with Christians in a world in which men are confronted with a multiplicity of religious and nonreligious claims to offer salvation. This necessitates the theologian's being able to communicate with non-Christians, to understand what they are saying. "Dialogue" is the overworked term for it today: it includes both listening and responding.

Because the relationship between the Christian community and the world cannot remain just intellectual and theoretical, theologians also should, through their writing and teaching, stimulate Christians to recognize their obligation to alleviate pressing social problems. In other words, a sign of the presence of viable theology in a given age is the degree to which the Church, institutionally and in its individual members, is contributing to the social welfare of persons. Theological reflection on social involvement, race and poverty problems, are necessary as reflective bases for Christian involvement, although they are no substitute for it.

We began this chapter with an expanded concept of faith. After explaining some of the elements of that concept in the context of sacred history, we discussed the question of interpretation. If faith is a claim to understanding, involving a selective interpretation of this world, the question of a norm for accuracy emerges. Whose theological interpretation is correct? A completely existential approach to Scripture tends to neglect the necessity for such a norm.

Having described the function and value of theology in relationship to faith, we have seen how the New Testament provides the normative witness to the experience of Christian faith as the community theologizes. We are now in a better position to reflect briefly on the nature of, and the necessity for, theological authority. What is the function of the magisterium, the teaching authority of the community?

6. MAGISTERIAL AUTHORITY

There is the necessity for some kind of criterion to assess the accuracy of Christian theologizing. The New Testament writings constitute a general norm, as we have seen. We have also discussed the partial but necessary function and value of theology in the lives of individual Christians and of the community of faith. There must be in that community individuals who can accurately assess the real questions of the day and who can relate the meaning of Christ's Revelation to those questions and questioners. There is need, in other words, for a kind of continuing criterion to provide that the inevitable propositionalizations of Christian faith do not obfuscate the understanding of faith for the members of the community. One component of Christ's promise that his community will not fail, that it will be "un-failable," must be the presence of some kind of teaching authority.

Obviously, no Christian can presume to claim that he possesses absolute certainty and truth in his faith. Faith is an acceptance of a person as well as an understanding of the world. But it does happen that Christians urge contradictory interpretations of the demands of faith vis-à-vis certain issues. How determine the accuracy of such demands?

Before proceeding to reflect briefly on the meaning of "infallible" teachings of the magisterium, it would be beneficial to indicate what the term does not mean. There has been much discussion of ecclesial authority lately, occasioned principally by the publication of *Humanae Vitae*. It is clear that the faithful do not exhibit a unanimity of belief concerning the nature and limits of such authority.

Theologians have been warning Catholics for some time that

infallibility should not be understood in association with the Pope alone. It has been so understood by many Catholics ever since the First Vatican Council. An understanding of infallibility which claims that the successors of Peter, the bishops of Rome, can periodically utter transhistorical jewels of immutable truth because of the promise of Christ recorded in the Gospel of Matthew is simply incorrect. That approach is too rigidly intellectualist, too pope-centered, to enrich the faith-experience of Christians.

A book which promises to become controversial in Catholic theology is one published in 1968 by the Most Reverend Francis Simons of Indore in India, a Roman Catholic bishop.[15] After careful analysis, the Bishop finds himself forced to concur with biblical exegetes such as Oscar Cullmann in the opinion that there is no scriptural evidence for the doctrine of infallibility as it is commonly understood by Catholics today. Any demonstration that such evidence exists would itself have to be infallible. Although he maintains the necessity for recognizing the presence of a teaching authority in the Christian community, the Bishop sees the present understanding of infallibility as an obstacle to Catholic growth, as well as to the progress of the ecumenical movement. Prescinding from the rather limited scope of the book, it is significant for many reasons, not the least of which is that its author is a contemporary Roman Catholic bishop, not an ancient heretic or polemical Protestant. This criticism arises from within the Catholic Christian community.

In the following brief analysis, our interest will lie in understanding what infallibility means in the context of our present discussion of faith and theology. No rigorous treatment of the doctrinal formulation, cited in the first chapter, will be undertaken.

It is best to begin with the promise of Christ to his apostles:

15 Francis Simons, *Infallibility and the Evidence* (Springfield, Ill.: Templegate, 1968).

"I will be with you for all days, even to the consummation of the world." The Christian believes that Christ's presence will prevent the community, on the level of existence, not just with respect to magisterial teaching, from ceasing to function as Christian community. Infallibility denotes the belief, based on the promise of Christ to be faithful to his community, that the community will not pass out of existence: that it will, through grace, be effective in bringing about the kingdom of God through redemptive love of men. Instead of concentrating on pope and teachings, this belief is oriented toward the whole people of God, and has to do with Christ's promise to maintain its existence.

Now, in order for that Christian community to continue in being as *Christian,* there must be individuals in each generation who are authentically Christian and who can articulate aspects of the experience of Christian faith accurately. There is the need, referred to above, to prevent the propositional aspects of Christian faith from becoming obstacles to Christians' faith. Such individuals must be able to recognize accurately the questions and problems of their time and to relate both the message and the demands of the Gospel to those questions.

Given the logical necessity for the presence of authentic teachers in the community, the problem now is one of recognition. How does the Christian ascertain which individuals are genuine teachers or prophets, and which are not? Christ indicated that there would be false prophets among the people of God. It is reasonable, therefore, that there be some kind of visible criterion for ascertaining the presence of authentic Christian theologizing.

Recall the language of the *Constitution on the Church* of Vatican I concerning infallibility: the Pope ". . . is endowed with that *infallibility with which* the Divine Redeemer has willed that *his Church*—in defining doctrine concerning faith or morals —*should be equipped*" (D. 1839) (Italics mine). The base of infallibility is the whole Church, the people of God.

The most important insight present in the definition, therefore, concerns a right and a duty. The Christian community has a right to expect, because of the promise of Christ, that the magisterium will not articulate aspects of faith in such a way as to inhibit their understanding of Revelation. The magisterium has the duty to serve the people of God, by clarifying the claims of faith vis-à-vis contemporary cultural situations.

For the fundamental nature of Christian authority is *service*. This is clear from Christ's words. "The Gentiles lord it over their subjects; but as for me, I have come not to be served, but to serve." Christ commissioned his apostles to exercise the authority of service in his community with the words, "Feed my lambs; feed my sheep." The Good Shepherd was he who laid down his life for his sheep.

It is clear that the Bishop of Rome occupied a unique position in the Christian community from the beginning. One indication of this is the fact that c. 90 A.D., while the apostle John was still living, the Corinthian community sought the counsel of Clement, the third Pope, in Rome, concerning a dispute.

The Pope, together with his bishops, because of their positions as successors of the apostles, are most recognizable in this regard. They are most recognizable, and should be authoritative in matters of Christian faith, because of their life-commitment to its implementation in the priesthood and episcopate. It is therefore reasonable to suppose that the teachings of the magisterium are more seriously worthy of consideration by the faithful than are the teachings of any random group of Christians. It is also true that the messages of other prophetic individuals in the community, though less formally recognizable, may be just as authoritative.

The magisterial body of the Church thus has the responsibility of clarifying the claims of Christian faith in contemporary situations. Because faith is most importantly a claim to recognize meaning and value in the world in terms of persons, the magisterium's responsibility consists in the obligation to recognize limitations and challenges to the fulfillment of that personal reality in the lives of men, and to redirect Christians to the task of safeguarding it. On some occasions or moments in the history of the Church, these recognitions and directions are most serious and constitute an obligation on the part of Christians either to accept them as true and binding or to investigate the sources of Christian tradition, unwilling to dissent except as a last resort of conscience.

This obligation of service on the part of the magisterium has been consistently exercised since the first centuries of Christianity. It has been exercised both solemnly and nonsolemnly. Every dogma of Christian faith, although formally referring to a unique topic, contains or implies this magisterial responsibility to safeguard the intrinsic dignity and value of human persons.

One example of such a dogma is present in the excellent book by David E. Jenkins, *The Glory of Man*.[16] In that book Dr. Jenkins develops his thesis that every doctrine has to be considered in its wider context, has to be dogmatically form-criticized, as reflecting a particular topical means by which the Church faces the question of its relationship with the world. The development during the first five centuries of the solemn teachings concerning Jesus Christ, culminating in the definition at Chalcedon in 451 A.D., is significant. Jesus Christ is one person, two natures; of one substance with the Father and of one substance with us. Such a statement is not only concerned with Christ. It was the magisterium's manner of expressing its attitude toward the world at the time. The Church fathers were emphasizing, in other words, that they held the world to be meaningful as the arena of God's personal and purposeful activity; that the locus of meaning and value in the world lies in the existence of persons; and that this affirmation and understanding is made possible only through the existence, life, teachings and Resurrection of Jesus Christ. The question at that time, in that context, is the same as is

16 Cf. Jenkins, *op. cit.*, ch. 3.

present in our own day: Is the world meaningful or not? Does human life make sense?

Examples of less solemn moments in the exercise of magisterial authority include the recent encyclical, *Humanae Vitae*. The encyclical must be interpreted in its historical context: today. What is there about this present historical context which could provide the magisterium with the necessity to recognize a challenge to human dignity?

Those who have viewed the film "The War Game" will not hesitate to agree that the nuclear threat is indeed one of those serious challenges. What does the nuclear threat have to do with *Humanae Vitae?* It is axiomatic to point to the determinative effects on human personality exerted by environment, both domestic and societal. Values and attitudes present in the home environment are assimilated by children in that home.

American children today are of the "television generation," exposed to an assimilating of information at a pace many times that of their parents and grandparents. Their home environment isolates and protects them from the harshness of life for a less extended period than was the case for previous generations of Americans. These children will be coming to maturity with an increasing awareness of the omnipresence of the bomb as a threat to human existence. Whether or not the final product of technology will be a mad generation of human beings, unable to cope with the foreboding presence of imminent destruction, present and future environments include that threat.

Young people, when considering marriage and family life together, are aware of this. Although no surveys exist yet, it is not difficult to understand why many young married parents make their decisions concerning the planning of their families with some awareness of the possibilities that their children will grow up in a desolated land, overpopulated and stripped of natural resources.

Humanae Vitae is consistent with the responsibilities of magisterial authority which we have been discussing. Exalting the dignity of the call to married life, the Pope calls attention to a fact which no one would deny: that the life of marriage and the raising of children are in fact closely related.

In a wider context, the Pope is counseling Christians to realize that the only way to provide for a healthier environment, one in which human values are safeguarded and promoted, is through the creative actions of persons. If environments determine persons, it is equally important to realize that human beings create the environments which in turn determine them. Future generations must be allowed the choice to interact humanly with their environments. Understood in this light, the encyclical presents the consistent magisterial obligation to call to mind and urge the recognition by Christians of their responsibility to live out what they profess to believe.

The statement by the United States Catholic Bishops in November, 1968, has joined statements by bishops of many other nations in allowing for, and urging the recognition of, still another basic human right and value: that of the exercise of conscience in matters of belief. That November statement remains consistent with those principles when it calls for an end to the nuclear arms race, a recognition of the right of Catholics to intelligent and competent dissent from reformable teachings of the magisterium, and a careful study of the question of selective conscientious objection to military service.

7. CONCLUSION

Christian faith is a claim to an accurate understanding of this world, human existence and the gracious Being of God; an understanding which is given in the being, life, actions and teachings of Jesus Christ; and one which calls for and makes possible the humanization of men and the worship of God the Father, in a community witnessing to the presence of his kingdom on earth.

This chapter has been an attempt to provide a preliminary explanation of that expanded description of faith, and to indicate the necessity and function of theology vis-à-vis the experience of faith. The remaining chapters will continue that attempt, by further specifying what is meant by the Christian claim concerning the meaning and value of human life in the world.

8. SUGGESTED READINGS

Revelation

Baillie, John. *The Idea of Revelation in Recent Thought*. New York: Columbia University Press, 1965.

Broglie, Guy de. *Revelation and Reason*. Trans. M. Pontifex. New York: Hawthorne, 1965.

Bulst, Werner. *Revelation*. Trans. B. Vawter. New York: Sheed & Ward, 1965.

Kuntz, John K. *The Self-Revelation of God*. Philadelphia: Westminster Press, 1967.

Latourelle, Rene. *Theology of Revelation*. New York: Alba House, 1967.

Moran, Gabriel. *Theology of Revelation*. New York: Herder and Herder, 1966.

Rahner, Karl. *Revelation and Tradition*. Trans. W. J. O'Hara. New York: Herder and Herder, 1966.

Schillebeeckx, E. *Revelation and Theology*. Trans. N. D. Smith. New York: Sheed & Ward, 1967.

The Theology of Rudolf Bultmann

Bultmann, Rudolf Karl. *Existence and Faith: Shorter Writings of Rudolf Bultmann*. Trans. Schubert Ogden. Cleveland: World, 1966.

——. *History and Eschatology*. New York: Harper & Row, 1962.

——. *The Theology of the New Testament*. Trans. Kendrick Grobel. New York: Scribner, 1951–55.

Ebeling, Gerhard. *Theology and Proclamation*. Trans. John Riches. Philadelphia: Fortress Press, 1966.

Henderson, Ian. *Rudolf Bultmann*. Richmond, Va.: John Knox Press, 1966.

3:THE WORLD'S MEANING IS PERSONAL / *the vision of Pierre Teilhard de Chardin*

We have seen some reasons for the failure in our day of the old apologetic as a way of demonstrating the reasonableness of Christian faith. Oriented primarily toward unbelievers and limited mainly to the question of the existence of God, this approach thrived on a concept of faith subtly prejudiced against the value of reason and defined almost exclusively in terms of God. It has demonstrated its inadequacy. The "arguments" of Christians with unbelievers and with men of other religious faiths simply do not interest many people anymore.

Beginning with the preceding chapter, we are attempting to sketch an outline for a new apologetic. The task of demonstrating the reasonableness of Christian faith is still necessary, although the project may be labeled by some as archaic. Such demonstration, however, depends upon the description of faith with which we have been working. Its value is for believers, not unbelievers. It is concerned with claims about this world and with human existence, not exclusively with God. It is an attempt to outline a matrix out of which Christians can integrate their visions of faith with their lives in the world.

It remains to explain further certain elements in that description; to attempt to indicate some of these "integrating possibilities" by discussing the faith-claims of Christians concerning Christ in language arising from the human observation of, and participation in, this world and human experience. For the Christian to make a claim about Christ is for him to accept a vision of the world and human life, as we have seen.

We have described Christian faith as a claim that the world is meaningful in terms of persons. Because such a claim is meaningful and points to concrete reality, evidence is relevant: evidence which tends either to verify or falsify that claim. It remains to be more specific about this "meaning": What is it?

Father Pierre Teilhard de Chardin, the Jesuit biologist and paleontologist, whose writings greatly have influenced contemporary theological world-views, provides a framework for specifying the Christian's claim about the meaning of the physical universe, a framework within which reasonable analysis and evidence are important. It is my purpose now, to summarize, interpret, and analyze aspects of that vision, in an attempt to specify certain claims of Christian faith.

There are many excellent summaries of the system of Fr. Teilhard de Chardin available, some of which are indicated in the suggested readings for this chapter. Thus my brief interpretation will be selective. The principal source for this section is his most influential work, *The Phenomenon of Man*.[1]

1. SCIENCE AND MAN

What is man? The scientist rejoices that the day is past when philosophers and theologians had complete and sole authority to answer this question. For the latter tend to bring unscientific presuppositions to such questions. For example, one philosophical approach would confront the question concerning man with the categories of "soul" and "body." Only in relatively recent times, in fact, have Western thinkers called those categories into question.

Today the scientific method demands that such questions be

[1] Pierre Teilhard de Chardin, *The Phenomenon of Man* (New York: Harper, 1959).

approached with as few presuppositions as possible. For example, the biologist, in his study of the living human body, would invalidate his eventual conclusions if he commenced that study with the presupposition that it is composed of matter and spirit. He must necessarily direct his study to men as they are, as phenomena, in terms of his particular method.

As Susanne Langer has indicated, this is an age of scientific specialization, beneficial in many ways—and yet potentially dangerous.[2] One of the problems is the communication of scientific information. It is no longer merely a case of chemists becoming so immersed in chemistry that they find it increasingly difficult to communicate with biologists and physicists equally immersed in their respective fields. Within each discipline, areas of specialization are becoming so minute and intense that there is arising a barrier to communications. Nuclear chemists are finding it more difficult to communicate with organic chemists, for example, although each positions himself somewhere within the field of chemistry. Consequently, the communications gap widens steadily among members of the various sciences, and between the scientific community and the rest of the human community. The symbolology of theoretical physics is less accessible to the average person than classical Latin, although the former is supposedly anchored in observable and testable phenomena.

One implication of this growing problem of communication, arising from increasing specialization within the scientific community, is that phenomena studied by all scientists become more partially accounted for. The account of man in a textbook in organic chemistry, for example, does not include elements present in a text in electrical biology. Both accounts demand ecological information, moreover; no organism can be understood apart from its environment.

The accumulation of more specialized data about man is beneficial. However, it is becoming apparent that there is a need for

2 Susanne Langer, *Philosophy in a New Key* (New York: Mentor Books, 1951).

scientific synthesizers who are sufficiently close to the methods and familiar with the disciplines to be able to contribute constructively to scientific intercommunication. These synthesizers would also be in a position to collate and evaluate the composite, "man," from the data arising from the various scientific studies.

Father Pierre Teilhard de Chardin is such a synthesizer.

A second danger arising from the ability of the various physical sciences to collect and organize data about man-in-his-parts has been present during the last two centuries. Some thinkers have shown the tendency, on the basis of the growing body of specialized scientific data about the human phenomenon, to form reductionistic conclusions. In other words, there is the tendency to conclude that the principles to which the terms "spirit" and "soul" referred in the past do not in fact exist. They are "spooks," philosophical by-products of an age in which man considered himself to be the spiritual center of creation, instead of an accidental waste production of a mindless galactic explosion-implosion. The human phenomenon can be "reduced," fully accounted for, by physics, chemistry, ecology and biology.[3]

The successes of specialized scientific studies of man, therefore, increase the temptation to conclude that the human phenomenon is reducible to the sum of its diverse parts and functions. Thus physics, biology and chemistry, along with ecological, sociological and mass-psychoanalytical analyses, can provide the complete picture of man.

For example, a person might conclude that the so-called spiritual reality of mind or soul is an epiphenomenon, and can be accounted for by explaining its activities in terms of electrical impulses. The brain is then a computer, exceedingly complex, but operating ultimately according to the laws of physics.[4] The

3 Cf. John Macquarrie, *God and Secularity* (Philadelphia: Westminster Press, 1967).

4 Sir Francis Walshe, "The Relationship Between Mind and Brain," in C. Talafous, ed., *Readings in Science and Spirit* (Englewood Cliffs, N.J.: Prentice-Hall, 1966), pp. 123–34.

higher is explainable in terms of the lower: the mind in terms of electrical charges and discharges.

2. COMPLEXITY AND CONSCIOUSNESS

Father Teilhard de Chardin was most anxious to make persons aware that a biological analysis of the human phenomenon, man, which either explicitly or implicitly presupposes reductionism, thereby restricting its interest and examination only to the external and measurable laws of recurrence in nature, is inadequate. Man must be approached by biologists phenomenologically, with as few presuppositions as possible. This involves the consideration of all possible data which contribute to understanding the phenomenon. By confining biological attention to the cells and organs of man, the scientist is not taking account of the total phenomenon.

For reductionism represents a value judgment, and arises as a possible conclusion, purported to rest upon the basis of scientific investigation. It is totally unwarranted and unacceptable as a presupposition. As such, it necessarily determines the results of scientific studies. To assume from the outset, biologically, that the human phenomenon can be completely accounted for in terms of the study of its parts and functions is to doom the study itself.

And this is the starting point: to notice that, along with the possession of extremely complex brains and central nervous systems, human organisms exhibit very high degrees of organic unity, demonstrated particularly in acts of consciousness. Men, besides possessing the most highly complexified material organs in the world of living things—their brains and central nervous systems—also exhibit the capacity for reflective thought, or consciousness. By whatever name chosen, the possibilities of abstraction, creation and choice point to an aspect of the human phenomenon not completely accounted for by the methods of the physical sciences. Thoughts cannot be measured quantitatively; they are not material.

This is not to predetermine the investigation of man from the outset. It is simply to make an observation, prior to any attempt to explain it scientifically. A scientific study of man which took no account of thinking would be incomplete.

Man, then, exists in at least two "aspects," both of which must be accounted for by the scientist who claims that his study is phenomenological. There is matter, present according to varying degrees of complexity, which is the "external," measurable dimension of man. There is also reflective thought-capacity, or consciousness, the "internal"; which does not operate, or at least may not operate, according to the same physical laws as the vital organs.

Again, it is not the application of a philosophical presupposition which leads to the conclusion that the "internal" activities of man do not reduce themselves completely to the laws of chemistry and physics. If everything a scientist said, for example, were ultimately reducible to explanation by the laws of physics, his claims about the truth of his statements would be meaningless. There would be no such thing as any human claim to truth. There would be only different statements about different topics, in each case totally determined by the laws of physics operative in the speaker. No one could acknowledge the claim to truth of any person—including he who claims that higher realities such as "soul" and "mind" are fictitious.[5]

If it is both accurate and therefore necessary to acknowledge the extensive influence of the physical organs, such as the brain, on the "mind," denying any kind of separate existence for the latter, it is also important to notice the reverse process. There are documented cases of Eastern gurus and Moslem fakirs who are able to stop their hearts temporarily, to cease their breathing for

[5] Cf. John Magee, *Religion and Modern Man* (New York: Harper & Row, 1967), p. 480.

days at a time. These feats are extraordinary indications of the influence which minds can exert on matter. Less distant and spectacular, but of the same order, as illustrating the same kind of influence, one only need study cases of maladies whose diagnosis reads "psychosomatic." From the small child desirous of missing an arithmetic examination on a given day, to the middle-aged hypochondriac acting from a basic insecurity and need to be appreciated, there are many examples in our everyday experience which point to the determinative effects of wishes and thoughts on human organic functions.

It should be noted that matter itself is a mystery. It is tempting, in discussions of the matter-spirit relationship, to presuppose an understanding of the concept "matter," and to focus attention on that elusive or fictitious "spirit," in attempts either to demonstrate its existence or to deny its reality. The atomic theory, which has influenced the entire discussion, has led some to consider matter to be composed of tiny, solid *particles,* as distinguished from space or vacuum. Yet, observations of matter on the level of atoms, electrons and protons seems to confirm the hypothesis that forces are the irreducible components of matter, not particles. On this level scientists observe, in the words of Sir Arthur Eddington, "something unknown . . . doing we don't know what." [6]

In the subsequent discussion, therefore, although language necessitates distinction, it is important to realize that the terms "external-internal," "matter-spirit," do not connote a dualism in reality. They rather connote, in the words of Father Teilhard de Chardin, two "faces" of a reality which is a unity. Our language is itself necessarily dualistic, even when utilized to describe a reality which is not. The "trick" is to use language in such a way as not to allow it to distort actual experience. [7]

[6] *The Nature of the Physical World* (London: J. M. Dent, 1935), p. 281. Cf. also Alan Watts, *The Book* (New York: Collier Books, 1966), pp. 101-28.
[7] For an excellent discussion of the neurotic basis and effects of language as such, cf. Norman O. Brown's critique of the Freudian study in *Life Against Death* (New York: Vintage Books, 1959), pp. 68-73.

It is necessary at this point simply to notice that men, as phenomena, seem to exhibit both material complexity and inward intensity, unity or thought-capacity; and to guard against a preliminary decision to ignore the latter before the evidence has been presented.

Beginning, really, with the work of the biologists Lamarck, Darwin and Mendel in the eighteenth and nineteenth centuries, there has been a growing tendency among scientists to accept evolution as providing a better account of living things than any other theory, such as the direct creation of everything by a creator-God. Higher forms of life, including men, have evolved from lower forms of life, selectively adapting themselves to their environments by means of complicated mechanistic processes not yet completely describable. Men have come out of the world, not into it.

Charles Darwin, in *The Origin of Species,* set the context by his observations for future investigation. For he noticed not only that living species exhibit a fundamental unity in terms of organic structure. He also claimed, in a creative hypothesis, a temporal insight: that higher forms of life present today actually evolved in time from lower forms.[8] In other words, prior to Darwin a kind of atemporal unity among living beings, in their cellular composition, had been noticed. Darwin's contributions included a temporal insight: that paleontological studies disclose less complex fossil remains which are older, the more deeply they are found in the earth's crust. Consequently, there is not only a unity and continuity among living forms, but a temporal progression as well. Lower forms preceded higher ones in time.

Father Teilhard de Chardin totally accepts the theory of evolution. Beginning with man, he notes the simultaneous presence of extremely complex organs, as well as highly intense interiority, or consciousness-capacity, as we have seen. Proceeding down the scale of living things, and backwards in time, he observes with Darwin that the degree of organic complexity decreases.

[8] Charles Darwin, *The Origin of Species* (New York: Mentor Books, 1958).

The brain and central nervous system of the German Shepherd, for example, does not exhibit the same degree of material complexity as the human brain and central nervous system. Yet with the German Shepherd, as with man, a biological study which is truly phenomenon-oriented will not limit its attention solely to the observable, external aspects, the without. The study will include the recognition that German Shepherds also manifest a kind of organic inwardness, or awareness—a within. Whether it is called "life-principle," "soul," or "within": the dog is a living organism, not just a particular conglomeration of atoms and molecules in a given environment. An examination of the corpse of a dog shortly after its death does not exhaust biological information about the canine phenomenon, data necessary in order to account for it.

Below the German Shepherd on the scale of life in terms of organic complexity, apparently preceding the dog in its appearance on this planet, is ragweed. At the level of plants it is evident that we are dealing with a degree of material complexity far below that which is present in man or in animals. Yet, there is present in plants a life-principle, an interior source of growth and reproduction by which the ragweed can assimilate gases and matter without destroying its cohesion. This within, although by no means approximating consciousness in man or awareness in animals, is nonetheless present, not accessible to instruments of quantitative measurement.

When the chemist breaks down organic molecules, plant or animal, he discovers cells. As he decomposes these cells into their tiny components, a point is reached at which the boundary between living and nonliving matter becomes so fine as to be nearly indistinguishable. But the simplest organic molecule demonstrates a degree of organizational complexity thousands of times more intense than the most complicated organic molecule.

Father Teilhard de Chardin is a groundbreaker in evolutionary theory because he was among the first to expand the theory of evolution to account for inorganic or nonliving matter as well as living material beings. As he proceeds down the scale of complex material beings, crossing the threshold between life and pre-life, he observes that the within of things becomes less obvious, more faintly perceivable. Consciousness, awareness, soul, life-principle: the inwardness present in varying degrees seems to disappear from view when we enter the realm of the preliving things.

Because the inwardness of things becomes less observable, however, it does not necessarily follow that it is no longer present in them at all. It is possible, in fact, to notice certain phenomena which indicate that such is not the case. Highly complex inorganic molecules, molecules whose atomic numbers approach one hundred, for example, exhibit a greater stability and inner cohesion than molecules with a lesser atomic number. The unity within molecules among the atoms becomes decreasingly intense as the molecules become increasingly simple. Consider the smallest imaginable atom (literally imaginable, not observable), which physicists tell us is composed of miniparticles such as electrons, neutrons, protons, mesons, positrons, et cetera. It is possible to make this observation: there seems to exist in the smallest components of matter an inward propensity toward unity with other matter.

Science students speak of the "attraction" existing between an electron and a proton. This term "attraction," as Bishop Berkeley was fond of pointing out, is not very scientific. The term is a metaphor. It arises from a relation between more complicated individual living beings much higher on the scale of life and being—human persons. It is applied analogously to the relationship between electrons and protons.

Based on the evidence available, it seems that there exists, as part or aspect of inorganic things and organic beings in the evolutionary process, a relational correspondence between the complexity of their material structures, and the degree of inward intensity, unity or stability. This degree of organic unity manifests itself as thought or consciousness in human beings. Beings manifesting the greatest apparent degree of material complexity on this planet (the human organisms) also give evidence most obviously for the presence of an inward intensity, life principle, or principle of organization, called consciousness.

Because scientific laws are supposed to be descriptions of actual phenomena instead of theories fabricated beforehand and imposed arbitrarily upon the evidence, it is possible to formulate the above observation in terms of a law: the law of complexity-consciousness. It states that the degree of material complexity of a being, living or nonliving, is directly relative to the degree of its inward intensity.

Another conclusion is warranted. There is some force in material things that causes the degrees of central organization or inward intensity—the source from within them of the propensity in particles and organisms to unite with others to form increasingly stable levels of unitary being. This force can be designated "radial energy." Its presence in the simple inorganic molecule is evidenced according to the strength and stability of the attractions and bonds among the atoms. In plants and animals that strength, stability, attraction and series of bonds contribute to the existence of what we have called the principle of life. Human beings are conscious megaparticles of nature's most complicated structures, and reflect on a higher level the same basic propensity to unite with other correspondingly complex beings for the sake of achieving higher levels of unity. Radial energy is the inherent force of the dialectical process of evolution.

The simplest material structures appeared earliest in time. Because the most complex material structures, men, came into existence only after billions of years of evolution, it would seem that a direction is discernible in that process. The process of evolution has been one which reveals a progression toward higher forms of material complexity and inward intensity.

This insight into the directionality of the evolutionary process is fundamental to the vision of Father Teilhard de Chardin, although it is regarded as an unscientific concept by other biologists. Father Edward MacKinnon, in a recent issue of *Continuum*, has pointed to the reluctance among scientists to include the category of final causality or purpose in their descriptions of phenomena.[9] As Julian Huxley has said, the scientific method may allow one to notice that certain phenomena in nature follow each other *as if* they were caused, *as if* natural processes themselves therefore exhibited a purposiveness or goal. But the concept itself is a logical imposition by the human mind on the phenomena. The concept of purposiveness does not arise from the phenomena. It is not immediately evident; thus it is not scientifically permissible.

One of the clearest dissenters to such a position is Dr. Charles De Koninck. In his book, *The Hollow Universe*, he utilizes Aristotelian metaphysics to show the value of the category of final causality as a necessary step in order to account scientifically for natural organic phenomena.[10] De Koninck analyzes the meaning of the term "organism," and shows that the essential component of the term is "tool." A tool implies purpose-in-order-to-fulfill-needs. A corpse, for example, is not an organism. It is simply a molecular mass with inactive appendages.

If, he reasons, it is possible to notice in nature that some processes are "good," and others "evil," then the point is clearer. For example, one can acknowledge that it is good for a man to be healthy, for all his organs and limbs to be integral and operative. It is good for flowers to bloom. Now, the ability to recognize and conceptualize what is good for beings becomes a more difficult task as one proceeds further down the scale of beings. What is good for a rock? But the presence of difficulty does not cancel the

9 Edward MacKinnon, *"Humanae Vitae* and Doctrinal Development," *Continuum*, Vol. 6, no. 2 (Summer, 1968), p. 274.

10 Charles De Koninck, *The Hollow Universe* (Quebec: Les Presses de l'Universite Laval, 1964), pp. 97–107.

necessity for the task itself. The only way to maintain that the question of purpose in nature is irrelevant is to be totally indifferent as to whether a result of natural processes is good or bad. It is difficult to account for everything in terms of chance, for chance itself implies purposive action in order to be a meaningful concept.

In fact, it is "final cause which establishes an intelligible connection between causes in nature." [11] Although biology must refuse to impose abstract and unscientific categories upon phenomena, it remains true that intelligible accounting for natural laws demands the recogition that natural phenomena exist and act for reasons—whether or not those reasons are evident. To deny this would be to affirm the unintelligibility of natural processes, a position which in itself is unscientific—if for no other reason than that it makes the scientific enterprise impossible.

Father Teilhard de Chardin, as a scientist, also claimed to recognize the presence of purposiveness in the evolutionary process. He noticed as well that the process as such, in order to continue, demands the power of an inward source of energy. Why? According to entropy, he claimed, which involves the dissipation of matter into forms of energy, this multigalactic system is "burning out," losing energy. Instead, the activity of the process of evolution, the production and development of increasingly complex forms of matter and life, indicates just the opposite. There is a discernible increase in the rate of cosmic activity, not a decrease. Conclusion: there must be present at the heart of the process a self-replenishing source of energy, sufficient to account for its consistent and ever-increasing forward progress against the tendency toward equilibrium (homeostasis). This is also radial energy.

So radial energy is the energy of the within, operative both within individuals and at the center of the process as a whole. There is in things an interior principle of dynamic unity which manifests itself increasingly in existing material beings as time

[11] *Ibid.*, p. 107.

unfolds. There is, in the process as such, a force or dynamism pushing it onward and upward.

3. BIOGENESIS AND NOOGENESIS

It is now possible to discern and discuss briefly the different stages of this process of evolution. As we have seen, evolution occurred on the level of inorganic matter at first, by means of beings demonstrating ever greater degrees of material complexity and inward intensity. Over a process of, probably, millions of years, the galaxies, planets and this earth were formed, whether by fissionary or fusionary processes.

There followed years of the development of elements, molecules and compounds, progressively externally complex and inwardly intense. An "envelope" of gases and matter was formed by the growing multiplicity and complexity of beings present in the atmosphere. It became more concentrated. The available space became saturated as the process of evolution began to exhaust its possibilities on that level. It began to produce inorganic compounds of such organization and inward intensity that the process as such reached the point at which more quantitative addition would effect qualitative change. This "envelope," in which these inner tensions kept rising, is called by Father Teilhard de Chardin, "cosmosphere." Cosmogenesis is the first level in the process of evolution—that of inorganic matter.

Why did quantitative addition effect qualitative change? The process reached, as it were, a "critical threshold," a point at which the inward tension, present as a result of the multiplicity and complexity of inorganic material things, reached such a degree of saturation as to demand a new level in the process of evolution. Some metaphors may be helpful in clarifying this point.

"The straw that broke the camel's back" is a familiar expression. When the number of straws had become such as to become a burden to the camel, a point was reached at which the addition of a single straw brought about an extraordinary result.

Water boils at one hundred degrees centigrade. When a beaker of water is brought to 99.9 degrees centigrade, and heat units are added one at a time, there arises that point at which the addition of a single heat unit brings about the transformation of the water into steam: quantitative addition brings about qualitative change.

Life is not yet capable of exact scientific definition. Although information about living things is accumulated daily, the term "life" has not yet been precisely defined. Proteins and viruses apparently share characteristics of both life and prelife. When, in the evolutionary process, cosmogenesis reached its critical threshold, its tension and "temperature" at the point beyond which the process could no longer increase quantitatively and not qualitatively, there occurred the leap to life, to living things, to the level of biogenesis.

Biogenesis is the second major phase or level of the process of evolution. From the simplest organic molecules, during a period of millions of years, increasingly complex living beings began to evolve, manifesting that relationship described by the law of complexity-consciousness. The same "theme" was played in biogenesis as in cosmogenesis, although in a higher octave.

Matter complexified and intensified. The most complex-intense level of matter possible in cosmogenesis remained as the substratum for evolution on the level of biogenesis. Cells, organisms, plants, fish, amphibians, reptiles, insects, vertebrates: within the process appeared beings of progressively complex material structures, with greater capacities for stability and growth. Living organisms exhibit more stability than preliving molecules. For organisms can ingest and digest, can assimilate new matter to themselves without destroying the bonds of unity among their constituent parts.

Biogenesis included the evolution, within the group of animals known as vertebrates, of many groups and subgroups, some of which became extinct. But the directionality toward more material complexity and inward intensity is most clearly evident in that group of vertebrates known as primates: the head-and-hand animals. In their brains and central nervous systems, matter reaches its greatest degree of complexity and intensity.

We now approach that point in our survey of the process of evolution at which biogenesis builds to its critical threshold. The life-envelope surrounding the prelife-envelope becomes saturated with a multiplicity and complexity of living forms, which begin to exhaust the possibilities of the evolutionary process on that level. Quantitative addition approaches the point at which another qualitative transformation must occur, among the most advanced group of living beings. The criterion or parameter for assessing the advancement of the process is, of course, the degree of cephalization, development of the brain and central nervous system, matter in its most complex-intense form.

There occurs another leap, to a new phenomenon: consciousness to the second power, consciousness squared. These megaparticles are not only aware; they are aware that they are aware. Consciousness turns in on itself, reflects, begins to build up the activities of abstraction and communication. The force of the entire process continues to complexify-intensify on the level of mind, of noogenesis, once more in a higher octave.

Evolution on the level of noogenesis does not appear to be progressing physiologically in the bodies, brains and central nervous systems of human beings. Does this constitute an end to the forward directionality of the process which has labored for so many billions of years to produce conscious megaparticles of matter? What can be the parameter to gauge the advance of the process on this level?

This is partly a question of judgment. For it is possible to maintain, with the French philosopher Henri Bergson, that the process of evolution, having reached the level of mind, now labors to make the individual centers of consciousness more intense in their individuality. Because personality, which includes self-consciousness, is the noogenetic phenomenon, the development from this point onward, some would say, proceeds inwardly: individuals whose growing brain activities and consciousness-potentials reflect measurable development.

Psychologists tell us that we function in normal daily life on a relatively superficial level of conscious awareness, never exercising all the consciousness-potential we possess. E.S.P., nonverbal communication, self-hypnosis, deep mediation—all represent areas of fascination and research in modern times. Cultural contact with the East has uncovered accounts of gurus and fakirs who exercise conscious control over their bodily functions far surpassing the normal control, as we mentioned before. Books and articles treating of poltergeists and demonic possessions recount strange events whose only plausible explanations seem to indicate the abilities of certain individuals to extend the powers of their minds beyond the limits of their own physical bodies.

The powers of consciousness do seem, if not to be growing, at least to be making themselves more evident in more people as history proceeds. Individual self-consciousness would naturally increase as powers of conscious awareness as such continue to do so. Yet individuation—individuals becoming more individual by increasing their consciousness-potential—explains only one aspect of evolution on the level of noogenesis.

On the levels of cosmogenesis and biogenesis two processes were in fact evident. Not only did inorganic and organic particles develop increasingly greater degrees of interior organization and stability, they also exhibited stronger tendencies to form complex unities through associations with other particles to establish (or reestablish) *unity*, not separation.

An example and a metaphor is the human body, in which we find an extremely complicated material unity. This unity is evident from two points of view: in the observation of the individual organs, and of the organism as a whole. Both approaches are necessary for the complete picture. The former would emphasize the fact, for example, that the human liver represents the highest development of "liver-ness" to be found among living beings. It is possible to proceed downward from human livers through the phyla, guided by the parameter of complexity-consciousness, and to notice that the further one goes, the less functional and stable are livers in living things. Finally the point arrives at which the liver in things simply disappears from observation, and we inspect less complex forms of life on the level of plants. Conclusion? The livers of human beings are the most developed and stable livers in the world. Similar observations could be made about other complex organs comprising the human organism.

This thought brings us to the second approach: apprehending the organism, not in terms of its separate parts, but in its inclusive unity. Although livers do not think and choose, they do function most effectively as livers when they are related to the other organs in the human body. A liver able to choose to concentrate simply on itself, not participating with other organs in the unified existence of the organism, would itself be unable to exist because the whole organism would cease to live. The liver could, of course, remain somewhat functional in a laboratory through artificial methods. But for a liver to be most effectively an individual liver, it must unconsciously and unfreely relinquish autonomous existence for the sake of participating in a higher form of unity not possible for the liver otherwise.

Both values, individuality and unity-through-relinquishing-autonomy, have been present in things from the beginning of the evolutionary process. On the level of noogenesis, consequently, it is necessary to expand our observation to include them. Acknowledging on this level, therefore, the increasing possibilities for individuation, while this is necessary and accurate, does not provide the total picture.

4. CONVERGENCE

Noogenesis also includes a gradual collectivization—the development of ever more complex forms of human community, which make individuation possible. Whether primitive human groups first appeared in the fertile crescent around Palestine and Egypt or in the valleys of Africa explored and studied by Dr. Leakey, it is fairly safe to say that men in their beginnings exhibited a rather tenuous pattern of social organization, not much above that of the apes or insects.

But there has been a fantastic development in this regard. From the caves and tribes, to the farms and small villages, to towns and cities, states and nations, to the relatively recent formation of the United Nations based upon the faint hope for, and recognition of the need for, a world community, men have formed a multiplicity and complexity of organizational relationships. Although the process has certainly not been unilinear, climbing in an unbroken line toward a world community, still the physical possibilities for such a community are finally present in our own time. If mankind manages to avoid self-immolation through nuclear warfare, individuals can continue to dream of that kind of community becoming real one day.

The parameter of the evolutionary process on the level of mind, therefore, is humanization: men becoming more human. This process includes the recognition not only of increasing personal individuation and consciousness-potential, which separate; but, more importantly, continuance in the development of complex and intense societal relationships among persons and communities of persons—which unite. The sociopsychic tension is increasing as the world becomes more populated. Noogenetic beings constitute themselves into nations, countries, leagues, power blocs. They create, partially by means of more advanced methods of transportation and communication, more numerous and more subtle relationships: religious, political, social, economic, intellectual, academic.

Information is disseminated through radio and satellite almost instantaneously throughout the world. Television brings important news events into the homes of millions of persons all over the globe. People learn of those events more quickly, as the interval between their occurrence and their dissemination decreases.

The process of evolution is moving toward "convergence," the formation of a human world-community, rather than "divergence," the formation of individuals simply as individuals. Human beings are one. Fred Hoyle, the noted physicist, has written a science-fiction novel entitled *The Black Cloud*.[12] The book as a whole is fascinating, but there is one strand which is particularly relevant to our present discussion. It involves the biography of the cloud. The cloud relates its past history, relating the time when it did not exist as a unity. Individual elements and particles existed within it, which communicated verbally with one another. As their means of communication became more efficient, as the interval between the actual conscious experiences of the particles and the communication of those experiences to other particles decreased, there came a point at which verbal communication became too slow. Through a kind of E.S.P., the individuals reached a point at which thoughts and feelings were transmitted instantaneously among the members. When one particle thought or felt something, it was immediately transmitted to the other particles. At that point the group of individuals became an organism: the cloud was born.[13]

The human body is the locus of a similar situation. The brain and central nervous system, which connects every cell in the body to a regulative organ, are a highly complexified system of intra-organic communication. It achieves a velocity of information-sensation-communication far exceeding that achieved verbally by men or machines.

As two persons grow in their knowledge and love of each other, their reliance upon words for communication decreases. Lovers communicate in silence, with glances and gestures. Moreover, experiments in E.S.P. and nonverbal communication are revealing new possibilities for human communication. The expectation

12 Fred Hoyle, *The Black Cloud* (New York: New American Library, 1954).
13 Cf. *ibid.*, p. 140.

that, with the formation of a world community, words will cease to provide the only means of human communication is not an unfounded one.

The pattern according to which human evolution has in fact unfolded gives evidence for describing this phase of the evolutionary process as convergence instead of divergence. Men are becoming more human, which involves both the values of individuation and communion. Both aspects of this humanization are strengthened by the successes of technology in creating the physical and mechanical possibilities for growth. More effective means of transportation and communication, not to mention medical discoveries and advances waging effective struggles against disease and death in many parts of the world, contribute to the creation of an environment which allows human beings to live humanly, recovering their unity, instead of waging hopeless struggles against the processes of nature. As educational processes and techniques improve, and the literacy statistics among peoples continue to reflect a rise, there is stronger impetus to accelerate this process of humanization or convergence.

Science and technology, then, as noogenetic activities, witness to the growing ability of human consciousness to put matter at the service of spirit, nature at the service of persons. There is no intrinsic opposition implied here. We are not considering spirit and matter to be separate entities. Realizing that according to the law of complexity-consciousness the degree of the within is directly correspondent with the degree of the complexity of the without, it becomes evident that the establishment of fruitful unity between matter and spirit has been present since the beginning of evolution.

5. THE DIALECTIC OF FREEDOM

On the level of inorganic matter, cosmogenesis, the within is very faintly present in things, almost totally eclipsed by the without. On the level of life, the within, soul, or life-principle obviously penetrates and permeates the matter in plants and animals more thoroughly. There is a coherence in which each is inseparable from the other.

Within that phase, in fact, it is possible to notice an ascent on the scale in the degree of determination-from-within of beings, proceeding from plants to animals. Animals reflect a greater degree of awareness, the ability to "choose" according to instincts and drives, the capacity to move about. It is on the level of mind, in noogenesis, that spirit most clearly permeates, or sublimates, matter. The living human body is matter which in our present experience is most clearly at the service of spirit. The fact that it is impossible to separate these two "faces" of reality in a living human being demonstrates the intricacy of their coherence in the human body. The face, the hands: living human flesh is matter coherently sublimated by spirit.

Painting, statues, skyscrapers, surgical tools, typewriters: millions of objects manifest less clearly but nonetheless really the service to which personal consciousness puts the material processes of nature. Obviously, technological progress is a key means for advancement in this regard. There is every reason to have confidence in continued progress and success. Genetic control techniques create the possibilities for men to extend their capacity for conscious control over matter into the crucial area of family planning, providing for the elimination of some hereditary defects and diseases. Obviously, this includes the risk of horrible consequences, as well, if the decisions to utilize this knowledge and those techniques do not reflect principles safeguarding human dignity.

These last observations bring us to a very important insight. We have described the essential components of freedom: the capacity for conscious self-determination. We notice one very important value which has emerged for the first time on the level of noogenesis—the future, as a significant factor in the experience of noogenetic beings, and a number of options arising as a result. The process, which moved ahead from the beginning through beings whose behavior was unconscious and unfree, now proceeds in the dialectic of freedom: conscious megaparticles with the capacity for self-determination, the ability to become more human.

Within the process has arisen beings who are conscious, not determined completely from without, capable of determining themselves from within. Matter on the level of cosmogenesis almost submerged the within. Living things more obviously act from their centers, from within. Consciousness gives things the greatest capacity for determination-from-within.

The continuing success of the process as a whole, therefore, is no longer automatic. It is a possibility, and demands conscious choices of conscious particles of matter. This point is perhaps clearest when expressed negatively. Besides the beneficial technological advances, human beings have created the means for the nuclear obliteration of all life on this planet. There are approximately three billion members of the human species. Nuclear armaments now in existence supply the equivalent of one hundred tons of T.N.T. for every living human person. As more nations supply themselves with nuclear warheads, the odds become greater that these weapons will indeed be utilized. Evolution now proceeds, dependent on the conscious choices of men. Men can use computers to improve the opportunities for people to live humanly, by putting natural processes more at the service of humanization; or they can use them to eliminate all living things and put an end to the process of evolution on this planet.

If the process of evolution is to continue its advance toward convergence, human choices must be in accord with the recognized values of humanization, not contrary to them. Individual persons must be set free to think, to communicate, to come to greater self-awareness and to recover their unity with one another. The community of men on the verge of being born must be

allowed to come to term. Freedom, for the individual human being or for the human community as such, consists essentially in
the ability for self-determination, in accord with the values of
individuality and community. For these values are fundamental.

This short analysis provides a criterion for assessing the worth
of human decisions and actions, considered socially or individually. The choices of a person are good if they reflect and enlarge
his capacity for self-determination, and if they contribute to the
humanization of other persons.

No man is totally free, or determines himself completely from
within. Behavioral psychology as well as commonsense observation reveals that the majority of everyone's decisions are determined significantly by factors outside his control. No individual
chooses the time of his birth, his parents, their values, the values
inherent in the societal structures in which he matures. One
necessary element in the process whereby a human being becomes
free is the recognition of the extent to which he is in fact determined. He must realize that the range of possible decisions available to him is in fact limited by factors beyond his control, the
reality-principle. It is necessary to be able to accept necessary
limitations and to work creatively within them.

No person is completely self-determinative. There is no one,
on the other hand, who does not determine himself at least somewhat. Father Karl Rahner has remarked that no person is free not
to be free to exercise freedom.[14] Psychologists remind us not only
that environments contribute to the formation of personalities,
but that persons contribute to the formation of environments.
Neither is intelligible alone. Every experience in the life of a person determines his life in some way, internally or externally. Some
choices, some experiences, are far more significant than others
and thus exert a more profound determinative effect. A choice
concerning a profession, for example, can effectively determine

14 Cf. Karl Rahner, *Mary the Mother of the Lord* (New York: Herder and
Herder, 1964).

the life of any person for many years. To become a fireman at the age of twenty-one is to rid oneself of a whole range of possible decisions concerning vocational goals which were previously present.

Working out of given situations, including environment responsibilities, past decisions and internalized values, persons do determine their lives. The choice to enter a marriage relationship determines a person's future, both his own continued internal development and the kind of environment within which he and his children will live. Choices themselves are determined significantly by past decisions.

Choices which unduly determine the life of a person from without are not freeing choices, but enslaving ones. Freedom is not merely the capacity to determine one's life from within. As we have seen, it also demands that such a capacity be actualized in accordance with genuine human values. The individual, for example, who consistently fears to make decisions, who chooses to avoid the risks of doing so, places himself more surely in bondage to his environment and to the decisions made by others which determine his life. Men's lives are determined, whether they themselves do so or not. A truly free decision is one which arises from within and which contributes to the formation of the self in accordance with the human values of individuality and community.

There is a further consideration. Allowing for the determinative influence of decisions on environment, and the communal nature of the lives of most human beings, it follows that the choices of individuals contribute in varying degrees to determining the lives of others. Perhaps the best example of this is the family situation, where the decisions made by the parents, decisions reflecting their values and goals, determine the environment and personality formation of their children. Experience reveals that some parents contribute to the humanization of their children by forming healthy and sound home environments, while others provide for the excessively repressive and neurotic psychic formation of their children.

"No man is an island." Because of the intense and complicated system of human interrelationships, all decisions, some more apparent than others, exert determinative influences on the environments of others. Presupposing this interdependence, a free choice demands that the resulting determinants not only contribute to the human growth of the chooser, but also that they do not contribute to the enslavement or undue external determination of other persons. The "pusher," who earns his living by "hooking" teenagers on narcotics, enslaves not only himself, but countless other individuals. Individuals unduly limit the evolutions of each other in millions of ways. This is why the process of evolution is advancing ambiguously, through suffering. Freedom for all persons becomes more possible as the physical possibilities for creating human environments increase. But the creation of such an environment is a possibility, not a necessity.

Existentialist philosophers emphasize that persons are not composites of impersonal substances such as bodies and souls. Rather, persons constitute themselves through their decisions; they make of themselves what they choose. The "self" is not a thing, implanted ready-made within a body at birth, only to emancipate itself at death. Rather, experience teaches us that selves come into being as the total result of acting upon, and of being acted upon by, their environments.

Any discussion of human responsibility, if it is realistic, must include the factors we have been discussing. Persons determine themselves not only externally, by contributing to the formation of environments determinative for themselves and for others; but internally, by progressively forming their own decision-making selves. A man whose decisions during a period of many years, for example, reflect a fundamental option of selfishness, self-at-the-expense-of-others, creates the likelihood that his future choices will manifest and strengthen that same concern. Father Yves Congar affirms the impossibility of "deathbed conversions." [15] There have been, apparently, complete changes of heart by persons in middle and old age immediately prior to their deaths; still it is psychologically impossible for a person who has constituted himself consistently in terms of selfish values to act suddenly according to selfless ones. He would have to be a different person.

The process of evolution has provided conscious megaparticles which have thus assumed responsibility for the future of the entire process. They are relatively conscious and free, having the capacity within their situations of determination to gradually transform their world into a place in which individuals can develop themselves and relate to each other, realizing their intrinsic unity. Technological advancement is an important element in this advance. Because ignorance unduly determines the possible choices available to persons, education and improved techniques of education are necessary, also. The better a person understands his world, the wider his range of possible choices. To know is to be free.

Whatever contributes to the process of humanization, providing for the freeing of human beings for interior growth and unity with each other, contributes to the success of the evolutionary process as a whole in attaining its goal.

6. THE PHENOMENON OF LOVE

Is it possible to discover the reality, present in noogenetic experience, which most evidently contributes to the humanization of persons? This reality must be one which unites persons interiorly. But it must unite them without destroying their personal capacities for interior development. As Gustave Thibon has said, mere comradeship is destructive of human personality. If everyone had the same name, wore the same-colored clothes, used the

15 Yves Congar, *The Wide World, My Parish,* trans. Donald Attwater (Baltimore: Helicon Press, 1962), pp. 87–89.

same words, such a fellowship would exist—but at the expense of persons. The reality necessary must be one which provides for the uniqueness of persons, enriching that uniqueness in the very act of binding persons together. It must be a reality which frees persons because it unites them at their centers. Nourished from their centers, it must be self-replenishing.

A glance backward and downward on the scale of evolution reveals that radial energy has been present since the very beginning, as the force providing for the degree of interior organization in things and for their proclivity to associate themselves with other beings in forming increasingly higher forms of unity. We earlier used the example of the human body to illustrate that point. In the body each individual organ reflects a degree of inward organization. Yet it also functions in harmony with the other organs and members of the body, thus participating in a degree of unity otherwise inaccessible to it. The human organism maintains a greater degree of inward intensity, in reflective consciousness, than any other evolutionary being.

Noogenetic megaparticles move to unite with other human beings, forming personal and social relationships which permit them greater participation in human life. But the "decision" by which beings on the levels of cosmogenesis and biogenesis safeguard their individuality while uniting with other beings is unconscious and unfree; while such decisions on the level of noogenesis must reflect both consciousness and freedom.

We have described now some of the necessary components of a reality which, as we have seen, is vital to the formation of a convergent society. It must be a reality by which conscious and free megaparticles inwardly unite with others in such a way as to maintain and enrich their uniqueness as personal beings. It alone conforms to the requirements necessary for creating a genuinely free and human environment. It is not a superfluous luxury, but a necessity, making possible the continued advance of the process of convergent evolution. The above description constitutes, from the point of view of evolutionary analysis, a phenomenological minidescription of *love*.

Radial energy, that force within unconscious and conscious particles and organisms which moves them from within toward greater degrees of complexity and consciousness, as well as toward unity with other beings, is love. Radial energy is present in things which are preconscious and prefree; when, in noogenesis, it becomes sublimated by freedom and consciousness it is love.

This cursory analysis of the world in the process of evolution has directed us to the realization that it is love which is the effective agency driving the process forward in accordance with the very values it has created. Love is not just a "nice thing to have," a way to live in order to get along with other people. It is a physical and biological necessity, indispensable for the evolutionary process as such to reach its term in the dialectic of freedom. The unity of brothers, not the simultaneous presence of comrades, is the reality which must be effected by these conscious particles. Love alone, in all its forms, unites beings at their centers while preserving and enriching that about them which is unique. Brotherhood as an ideal is capable of attracting conscious and free persons in a way that comradeship is not. For comradeship rests as an ideal on the impersonal abstraction of "mankind," while brotherhood is an experiential reality which builds upon and strengthens personal unity.

Love, which by description as well as by experience includes both consciousness and freedom, can appear only on the level of noogenesis. But it is prefigured on the other levels, as consciousness and freedom themselves are prefigured and prepared for. In fact, Fr. Teilhard de Chardin refers to the attraction among tiny miniparticles of matter, that inward propensity to unite with other particles, as "prelove."

As we ascend the scale of evolution from cosmogenesis toward noogenesis, we encounter relationships among living beings which begin to resemble the love relationships appearing between and among organisms on the level of mind. When sexual reproduction first appears noticeably on the level of plants, and more evidently among animals, the relationships at least faintly resemble love relationships existing among human beings. The devotion of the dog and the horse to their masters, the intricate relationships constituting the familial lives of porpoises or baboons, the monogamous relationships between male and female wolves—all these precede and prefigure the conscious and free personal relationships of love among persons.

In our experience, love prepares for and creates its own possibilities. In the family situation, for example, the love of the parents for their child can become complete only when the child develops psychologically to the point at which he can recognize and respond to that love, consciously and freely. His parents' love is present from the beginning of his life as an important determinative factor in his environment, as the motive for their care for him. But love unrequited is only partially effective. The child must mature and enlarge his ability to return that love before it is as effective as it is meant to be.

As a young man and young woman come to know each other better, and grow more deeply in their love, their capacity to love each other deepens. In this case also, love is a reality which creates its own possibilities.

This is true for the process of evolution as such. Radial energy, coherently sublimated by consciousness and freedom on the level of mind, is love. It has been operative from the beginning, creating the possibilities for its coming-into-being. Once again we encounter the concept of retroactive revelation. The higher and later beings in the process retroactively reveal the significance of the lower and earlier. It is only on the level of mind that the direction of the process as a whole can for the first time be recognized. The lower stages can now be seen as preliminary to, preparatory for, and prefigurative of, the higher stages.

7. REVELATION AND THE FUTURE

"Retroactive revelation" refers to the fact that it is from the vantage point of mind alone that, for the first time, evolutionary beings can recognize the direction of the process and can discern the values inherent in that process: values which must be implemented in order for that process to continue in the correct direction. The billions of years during which the process labored through cosmogenesis and biogenesis, during which billions of inorganic and organic beings came into existence, were for the sake of reaching the level of mind. Mind is therefore dependent upon the lower levels of being for its ability to exist and to function.

The first living thing demanded an extremely high degree of material complexity in order to support the degree of inward intensity known as life. The degrees of inorganic and organic complexity must be extremely high in order for there to be consciousness. So also, the degrees of inorganic, organic and conscious life must be sufficient for the next leap to occur. Conscious particles are creating the degree of humanization necessary as a prerequisite for the next leap, by creating the possibilities for world brotherhood and by actualizing these possibilities in their own lives through love.

Thus the retroactive revelation of the significance of the process has implications not just for the past. It also provides a basis for some partial knowledge about the future. For the most advanced beings on the level of cosmogenesis are the basis for evolution on the next level, that of biogenesis. The most advanced biogenetic beings were prerequisites for the leap to, and the development of, noogenetic beings. If the process as such remains faithful to its own principles, it becomes possible to predict that the next level, that following noogenesis, will safeguard and build upon the highest degrees of inorganic, organic and psychic (individual and social, conscious and free) life as a basis for further development.

Convergence thus means that the process of evolution is tending toward a goal, one which is becoming more discernible with the passage of time. This goal must be one which safeguards the highest values of all levels. Father Teilhard de Chardin calls this goal "Omega Point": hyperpersonal being, around which the human community will gather in consciousness and freedom, in a dynamic state in which matter is totally at the service of spirit. Omega Point coherently sublimates the three lower levels of cosmogenesis, biogenesis and noogenesis. Omega must be at least personal, because an impersonal goal would be incapable of safeguarding personal uniqueness, as well as attracting free and conscious megaparticles through love to form the true unity which is required. As we have seen, progress toward the goal of the evolutionary process is no longer automatic. It must come in the dialectic of freedom: as a result of the conscious and free choices of human persons. This demands that there must be a goal capable of attracting persons so strongly that they interiorly bind themselves to one another in order to achieve it. External coercion into a condition of comradeship cannot be the means for attaining Omega. Omega must be both immanent in, and transcendent to, the process as a whole: present faintly since the very beginning, creating the possibilities for its effective recognition, as the source of a reality revealed on the level of mind, the reality of love. As a human person coherently sublimates matter by means of life, Omega is meant to coherently sublimate conscious megaparticles by means of love. But the formation of this hyperorganism must come about through the free choices of the individual cells and organs, made in order to achieve unity.

Father Teilhard de Chardin proceeds to describe Omega in much more detail. He gives it a name, "Christ," explaining the necessity for the immersion of Christ-Omega into the process itself. Christ, as the retroactive Revelation of the process on all levels, reveals their intelligibility. Recognition of the be-ing of Christ by noogenetic beings is therefore impossible without understanding his intrinsic relationship with all levels of reality. Accepting Christ in faith is accepting a certain vision of all reality, making the claim that it is meaningful and valuable in terms of persons. More will be said in development of this in Chapter Five.

The significance of the evolutionary process is clarified on the level of mind, thereby providing a criterion for assessing the relative value of human decisions. It is important to realize that love alone can bring about the kind of progress indicated by the process of evolution itself. It is a matter of necessity, not of luxury. There are various goals present today, implicit and explicit, urged by individuals and by groups, which call for the commitment of human beings. It is the extent to which a given ideal really safeguards important human values that provides the criterion by which to evaluate it.

8. CONCLUSION

Father Teilhard de Chardin, as I indicated earlier, identified Christ-Omega as the reality within the evolutionary process most clearly revealing the significance of that process. As a scientist, he maintained that in the future men would recognize that science and religion are two sides of the same coin: both being methods by which to make sense of the world and humanize it. He pointed to a "coherent sublimation" in the world by which organic matter continually elevates and transforms inorganic matter; by which conscious megaparticles continuously elevate and transform inorganic and organic matter; and by which Christ-Omega continuously elevates and transforms the world and human persons into a convergent community under God the Father. Men are one with each other—and with the whole of material evolution.

Christianity and the world are mutually interdependent, he taught—each existing for the sake of the other. Christians must therefore involve themselves in the processes of humanization prior to and preparatory for their works of formal evangelization. There exist no dichotomy, no orders of being completely independent of one another.

Father Teilhard de Chardin reflects the ability to integrate his Christian faith with his life. But notice that he does not look skyward to do so. He looks into this world and speaks meaningfully about it, offering evidence for his contentions. To be a Christian means first of all to be human and to engage in a life which contributes to the abilities of other persons to live humanly. His Christian faith was meaningful to him, partly because it made so much sense in terms of his analysis of the world.

"This world is meaningful and valuable in terms of persons." This statement should now be more intelligible. We have attempted to specify its meaning by looking at the phenomenon of the world in its process of evolution. Evidence counts. The evidence furnished by the world-in-evolution, gathered, related and articulated by Father Teilhard de Chardin, tends to confirm, rather than to falsify, that very important claim of Christian faith. And if that claim about the world and human life is false, then anything that could be said by Christians about God is also false. Integrating faith with life need not be a futile attempt to prove the existence of an inaccessible God to anyone not willing or able to accept that. It is a Christian task: it demands the ability to take rational account of human experience in this world in accordance with the vision of Christian faith.

The world is meaningful and valuable in terms of persons, because from the beginning the evolutionary process has labored to produce conscious megaparticles of matter, who have assumed the responsibilities arising from the possession of freedom. The precise meaning and value of personal existence is love, because that is the only reality which both unites and preserves personal uniqueness. The process itself reflects those values.

Is it possible to go further? Is it possible to speak meaningfully, in categories of human experience, to integrate the fundamental insight of Christian faith, and specify further the kind of love that it proclaims to be necessary? This question provides the subject of the next chapter.

9. SUGGESTED READINGS

Teilhard de Chardin, Pierre. *The Divine Milieu.* New York: Harper & Brothers, 1960.

——. *The Future of Man.* Trans. Norman Denny. New York: Harper & Row, 1964.

——. *Hymn of the Universe.* Trans. Simon Bartholomew. New York: Harper & Row, 1965.

——. *Man's Place in Nature; the Human Zoological Group.* Trans. Rene Hague. New York: Harper & Row, 1965.

——. *The Vision of the Past.* Trans. J. M. Cohen. New York: Harper & Row, 1966.

Francoeur, Robert T. *The World of Teilhard de Chardin.* Baltimore: Helicon Press, 1961.

Faricy, Robert L. *Teilhard de Chardin: Theology of the Christian in the World.* New York: Sheed & Ward, 1967.

Kopp, Josef V. *Teilhard de Chardin: A New Synthesis of Evolution.* Glen Rock, N.J.: Paulist Press, 1964.

Mooney, Christopher F. *Teilhard de Chardin and the Mystery of Christ.* New York: Harper & Row, 1966.

Murray, Michael H. *The Thought of Teilhard de Chardin: An Introduction.* New York: Seabury Press, 1965.

North, Robert G. *Teilhard and the Creation of the Soul.* Milwaukee: Bruce, 1967.

Raven, Charles E. *Teilhard de Chardin: Scientist and Seer.* New York: Harper & Row, 1962.

Tresmontant, Claude. *Teilhard de Chardin: His Thought.* Trans. Salvator Attanasio. Baltimore: Helicon Press, 1959.

Teilhard Conference, Fordham University, 1964. New York: Fordham University, 1964.

4: THE LIFE OF FAITH / *further integration*

In the last chapter, by means of the vision of Father Teilhard de Chardin, we specified the meaning of the Christian's claim in faith that the world is meaningful and valuable in terms of persons. Christians can and must direct their attention to this world in order to see the relevance of their faith to their life.

Some of the conclusions which emerged in the last chapter have been accepted by humanists and by other persons not formally Christian. These persons can acknowledge the world as thus meaningful, and they claim to recognize brotherhood as the specified goal of the evolutionary process. What is specifically Christian about that realization? How does Christ fit in? In what way is Christ necessary for the realization of this goal?

1. NONRELIGIOUS SALVATION?

It is an understanding of the existence and depth of evil, balanced by an awareness of the presence of grace, which constitutes one of the "differences" Christian faith makes to Christians. This is not to say that Christians should not realize that they share some important elements of their faith with all men who truly endeavor to implement the love ethic in their lives.

"Christ is God." This is a propositional expression of one important element in Christian faith. Why must a person believe that Christ is God, in order to be able to live out the vision, for example, of Father Teilhard de Chardin? What does it mean to claim that Christ is the Redeemer of mankind? Why is he Redeemer in such a special way? Can that element in our description of faith be integrated with the rest of life, in categories arising from human experience?

Signs near the highways in many states read, "Jesus saves." They point up the problem to which we are referring. The novels and short stories of J. D. Salinger and Flannery O'Connor express an uneasiness among contemporary Americans with language apparently urging a kind of maudlin self-deprecation upon men. We live in an age in which men have need for fewer "crutches." Dietrich Bonhoeffer reacted violently against the Christian institutions for their attempt to make the important questions of suffering, weakness and death into "religious" questions, seeking to gain men's allegiance by providing answers for the diminishing number of "ultimate" questions not yet soluble in scientific terms.[1]

Bonhoeffer spoke of "clerical subterfuge" in the churches. He meant that religion has convinced normally happy, healthy human beings that they are radically insufficient and depraved, after which it has proceeded to prove crutch-solutions, such as sacraments and the hope for an afterlife. "You are fundamentally corrupt and depraved, my son. Your sense of well-being is in itself a deception, a sign of your hopeless condition. Admit to yourself that you are sick, and accept the spiritual 'medicine' which I can offer you." Such an approach nourishes itself on the needless suffering of men. Bonhoeffer concluded his repudiation of "religion" by calling for the nonreligious interpretation of biblical concepts, by which he meant, in essence, that the churches should stop talking about God and start serving men more effectively. Christ, the man-for-others, does not provide the motive for "spiritual incest," for the churches to become so concerned with justifying their own worth to themselves that they fail to implement the mission of Christ in the world.

There is much validity in Bonhoeffer's critique of religion. Religion is not faith. But the solution lies not in ceasing to speak of God or of faith as such. It does not suffice to dispense

1 Cf. Bonhoeffer, *op. cit.*, pp. 160–70.

with a belief in the divinity of Christ as a prerequisite for ac-knowledging the reality of his humanity. If that is true, then it remains to indicate some ways in which a belief in the divinity of Christ is necessary and relevant to the lives of Christians in the world. Is it possible to speak "nonreligiously," that is, in a way which is meaningful on the basis of human experience as well as "religious" experience? What does it mean to say that Jesus saves? And what difference does it really make for Christians to believe that Christ is divine? Is it not possible to accept the ethic of love, and consider Christ a great moral leader, of the ilk of Gautama Buddha, Krishna, Mohammad, Gandhi or Martin Luther King?

In terms of our description of faith, this chapter will concen-trate on explaining the phrase, ". . . which calls for and makes possible the humanization of men and the worship of God the Father in a community witnessing to the presence of his kingdom on earth." To repeat once again the description of faith with which we are dealing: Christian faith is a claim to an accurate understanding of this world, human existence and the gracious Being of God; an understanding which is given in the being, life, actions and teachings of Jesus Christ; and one which calls for and makes possible the humanization of men and the wor-ship of God the Father in a community witnessing to the pres-ence of his kingdom on earth.

2. OBJECT-SELF AND SUBJECT-SELF

"Know thyself." To realize this Socratic axiom is perhaps the most difficult task for students in world religions courses, in attempting to understand the faiths of other men, especially those in Eastern religious traditions. It is necessary in the course of such studies to understand what is affirmed and what is de-nied about human personality. The problem presents itself most forcefully in a study of the Buddhist doctrine of *anata*, or no-self. The Buddha, anticipating in some ways the approaches of contemporary behavioral psychology, accounts for human individuals by means of impersonal forces in continual change. He denies the real existence of any kind of ego, person or self behind or beyond these impersonal forces of matter, feelings, impulses, perceptions and acts of consciousness. Just as "chariot" is a logical reality existing only when certain components are brought together in a certain way for a given length of time, so also "I" am a figment, a fictitious creation having no being independent of my thoughts, sensations, matter, feelings and impulses. Just as the chariot ceases to exist when its parts are obliterated, so also, when the impersonal forces contributing to my existence as an individual cease, "I" will not longer exist. For "I" do not really exist right now.[2]

It is this "I"-involvement in this world and in life which is the cause of suffering and pain, for me and for others. The goal of life, consequently, is the dissolution of this selfish craving, the arrival at an enlightenment which includes the realization that "I" am not, and the resultant abolition of pain and suffering. The Buddha himself provides an eightfold path as the way to attain this enlightenment to enter Nirvana.[3]

In a similar manner, the student of world religions encounters in the Hindu tradition, in his study of the Upanishads or Vedanta, the basic teaching that Atman is Brahman. There is an underlying reality in all things, a "ground of being," the basis for all becoming and process. This underlying reality is the same in all things, identical with the ground of being, the absolute. Egos are mechanisms of fictitious isolationism. What is most important about me is that I am Atman, I am Soul. And you are the same. Soul is Brahman-Absolute, playfully hidden in this world of illusion.[4]

2 Cf. E. Conze, ed., *Buddhist Scriptures* (Baltimore: Penguin Books, 1967), pp. 147–51.

3 *Ibid.*, pp. 112–16.

4 Juan Mascaro, ed. and trans., *Upanishads* (Baltimore: Penguin Books, 1965), pp. 117–18.

Again, in this context, those realities which we identify as ourselves are fictions, keeping us from realizing our identity with one another, introducing imaginary and divisive factors into our existence. Ignorance of this interior identity is the cause of all suffering and pain. Salvation consists in attaining an intuitive realization, not a logical understanding, of the truth that Atman is Brahman, that "thou art God," in the words of the Chandogya Upanishad.

In their study of Islam, students encounter the same basic teaching: that egocentricity is the principal cause of evil in the world. The ego must be renounced. A man must live a life of Islam, total submission to the Qur'an, the will of God. Egocentricity is abolished only through total submission, in placing onself totally at the disposal of Allah.

These same students, in their psychology classes, continuously encounter objections to an understanding of human personality which is too static and essentialist. In other words, it is obvious that so much about us, including memories, values, relationships, imagination, does change. An attempt to understand personality in atemporal categories is therefore inadequate. Some students, in attempting to relate what they have learned in their various fields of study, begin to lose the capacity for self-identification. The most basic question of all, one which meets incredulity and ridicule in people outside the university atmosphere, who live the "real" life, arises as a painful problem for these students: Who am I?

What kind of continuity exists between the small child who threw regular temper tantrums twenty years ago, and the college graduate seeking employment or planning marriage today? Although they call themselves by the same name, how correct is it to say that they are the same "persons"?

Physically, they are almost completely different. The six-foot Hercules of today barely resembles the pudgy little urchin of yesterday. "Body" is not a definable *thing*. It is a constantly changing process of matter. In other words, bodies do not remain the same. Everyday some of the matter constituting the body of every person dissipates into heat energy, while other matter enters to replenish the person at mealtime. The "molecules" composing the body of a person at a given moment are not those which comprised the body of that person seven years earlier. There is no necessary relationship between a person at a given moment in his life and the actual matter present in his body at that moment. There is a relationship of some kind, but one which includes the fact of molecular changes with the passage of time.

There is also psychological development. The twenty-year-old reflects a development in his personality, character traits, values and goals between the ages of three and twenty. We find ourselves now in an area of almost unimaginable complexity. Without becoming excessively technical, however, it is possible to make some progress toward understanding in terms of experience, and to point out some distinctions.

There is almost nothing about a person which, when subjected to introspection, does not reveal itself to have changed. But the twenty-year-old can still say, "When I was three years old. . . ." As his life progresses, and his experiences mount, it becomes evident that there is something about him which provides a continuity from day to day, and year to year. Although he might attempt to describe all his experiences during a single day to a friend, there remains the fact that the one experienced certain things, while the other did not. Even should his friend reach the point at which he could speak as exhaustively about the experiences as he who had experienced them, there still remains that difference between the participant in an experience, and the observer of it.

It is in speaking about memories that it becomes difficult to account for the ways in which the experiencer and the observer relate them, without allowing for the existence of some enduring center of conscious activity which unites from within the almost countless number of discreet moments constituting the life-span of an individual. "I" experience events in a manner different and distinct from that of any other person. How is it possible to account conceptually for these two factors of human experience: continuous growth and development, and some kind of continuous identity transcending discreet moments in time?

There is an important distinction present in the writings of certain Eastern and Western thinkers. From the Sufi mystics of Islam to the American philosopher-psycyhologist William James, sages have distinguished between a "higher" and "lower" self, a "once-born" and "twice-born" self, a "subject-self" and an "object-self." It is necessary to clarify this distinction, because it is pivotal for the experience of Christian faith-integration, providing a workable conceptual framework.

"I think myself to be basically an honest person." "I was amazed at myself." "I am disgusted with my behavior at the party." "I consider myself responsible for what happened." These statements share one presupposition: that there is a distinction, though not a separation, between the "I" in the first part of the statements and the "my" or "myself" in the second. It is especially evident in experiences of moral responsibility, or examinations of conscience, as well as in most introspective experiences, that the "self" observed as an object of conscious analysis is not totally identical with the analyzing subject.

These are intuitive experiences, granted. We intuit, as persons, the distinction between the self-as-object and the self-as-subject. We do so when, in experiences of moral responsibility, we hold our "selves" up to critical analysis and judgment. There is an "I" which is judging, there is a "myself" which is judged. No person is totally aware of himself at any one time. Most of his drives are unconscious. The self accessible to introspection, or to the observation of others, does not exhaust the reality of the person. No person, as Fichte maintained, can completely objectify himself to himself.

Self-hypnosis is an area of experimentation which is becoming more widely known, and which is revealing amazing psychic capacities in human beings. "I hypnotize myself; I put myself into deep meditation." Again, there is the self acting, the self being acted upon. The self acting, however, is completely subject; it is never the object of introspection.

In an experience of moral responsibility, a person reflects upon his behavior over a period of time in a certain context. "I was wrong; I am ashamed of myself." The subject-self pronounces an interior judgment on the object-self. But the existence of the subject-self is never known directly, through introspection. Otherwise, it would be object-self. It is intuited, recognized as having acted in past situations, rather than being observed or inspected in the present moment. The subject-self is totally subject, never object, either to the person himself or to others.

This distinction is crucial for what follows. Thus I must make myself clear. It is possible to prescind from technical Freudian psychoanalytic categories of personality such as "id," "animus," "superego," and ask the reader to reflect on his own experience, and to recognize the intuited distinction between the "I" and "myself." We can distinguish experientially between the subject-self, intuited only indirectly, as having acted, and the object-self, the many aspects of the personality capable of analysis and observation by oneself and by others. Synonyms for the object-self in the discussion which follows are "ego," "role," and "mask." It is this "ego" or these "masks" which are most immediately present upon introspection or observation.

We spoke previously of the difference between friendship and comradeship. There are many degrees in the unity which persons achieve with one another. There are some persons with whom we are only casual acquaintances. We have been introduced to them, and have shared a few amenities. When we find ourselves with such acquaintances, persons whom we do not know well, the dialogue often consists of "conversation" or "small talk." No one would claim that in such situations anything profound is occurring. There is, strictly speaking, no unity between these two persons, though there is a union. Two individuals are locally present at the same time. Neither would claim to be acting completely from the center, speaking from his own heart to the heart of the other. Rather, the relationship on this level is superficial. It is superficial, not in the pejorative sense of the term (although it may be that also). It is superficial because persons require time to get to know each other, to establish a unity, center-to-center, between them. At the party two egos encounter each other, manufacture conversation and exchange pleasantries. There are no ties, no commitments. Neither person is vulnerable to the other. Neither exposes himself to pain and rejection.

It is of course necessary for two people to meet each other for the first time. They must indulge in light conversation. Meaningful relationships develop slowly. Relating self-to-self, center-to-center, uniting with a person, together, instead of merely there at the same time: reaching this point requires time and effort, joy and suffering. The masks must fall.

Subject-selves are meant to utilize the egos and masks to make preliminary contacts with other selves, to make conversation and share sociable intercourse. Sociability is not a bad thing in itself. It is necessary as a means of preliminary encounter between persons, prior to and preparatory for possible interior unity. Egos are "polite," sociable, agreeable. They are functional, meant to be used to establish contact between persons.

Only rarely do persons get to know each other immediately. Friends, in recalling their first meeting with the person who has since become very close to them, realize how superficial was their knowledge of this very special person at their first meeting. For growing in friendship involves the ability and the desire to recognize and penetrate more of the masks which previously separated the two. So it becomes increasingly difficult to describe a friend verbally.

In other words, to describe Bill as a shallow person is satisfying only to persons who have observed Bill from a distance or met him casually. Bill's wife might well recognize that he sometimes impresses others as being shallow, but she is much less likely to utter one sentence, containing one adjective, as a total description of Bill. It is much easier to choose a trait as essentially descriptive of a person if one does not know the person well. The better and more accurate one's knowledge of a friend, the less adequate are words and phrases in describing him—especially to a person who has never met him at all.[5]

We ourselves experience a similar sensation when we hear pithy descriptions of our own personalities offered by others. First of all, we take more seriously descriptions of ourselves given by our friends. They know us better and are less likely to let the nonessential aspects of our personalities, the masks, the object-selves, hopelessly obfuscate their knowledge of us.

We may sometimes indulge in describing other persons in terms of a superficial impression or observation, based upon a reaction or small number of reactions which we have had to them. But we greatly resent other people taking the same liberties with us. "Jim is a liar" may be perfectly acceptable to us in a conversation, as a description of a person we do not know well. But for others to conclude that *I* am a liar, just because I have toyed occasionally with the truth, strikes me as unfair and reprehensible. I rebel at the proclivities I recognize in others to identify me, my essence, in terms of what I sometimes do, my actions. I live with the recognition that my deepest self is not available for observation by others; that what they notice about

<hr />

[5] Cf. Gabriel Marcel, "My Life," in R. Caponigri, ed., *Modern Catholic Thinkers,* Vol. 1 (New York: Harper & Row, 1960), pp. 109–23.

me is not the total me. But it is too easy sometimes to forget that distinction in conversations about others.

The better we know ourselves and other persons, the less adequate becomes description verbalized completely on the basis of observed reactions. In fact, the more adequate our knowledge of persons, the less adequate are words; they simply do not do the job.

Relationships begin on the superficial level, that of masks, impressions, the object-selves. It is in this manner that persons establish contact with one another, without exposing themselves to real pain or joy. This is the preliminary step on the path to the development of a personal understanding, a unity between persons center-to-center, a love relationship in which persons are vulnerable to one another.

This raises a further point. The masks perform another function, besides establishing preliminary contact with other persons. They also provide a buffer zone between the world of shared experience, the everyday world, and the world of the subject-self. The self must protect itself from pain. The most painful human experience is rejection, knowing oneself, not just a mask or a role, to be rejected.

Self-rejection is always painful, although the degree of pain is relative to the degree of subject-self-presence. To illustrate this point, consider the classroom situation. Many students attend university classes for four years, pass their regular examinations and graduate with the A.B., without speaking extensively or at all during any class period during all that time. Some students, during a classroom discussion of an issue to which the offering of personal opinions is pertinent, cannot force themselves to speak. Why? In offering one's opinion on an issue, especially an important one, the person is involved. He has a stake in what is being said. The experience of speaking out includes accepting the risk that others in the class will laugh or scoff. And that is painful. Silence is the solution, for it prevents that painful rejection-experience. The classroom situation is never deeply profound, never involves the total subject-self. But it occasionally demands making oneself slightly vulnerable, risking pain, ridicule and suffering.

The risk increases, moreover, with the degree of self-presence in situations. The most painful experience in human life is that of taking the risk of rejection with another person, of letting that other person completely inside, of tearing down all the masks and facades—and of being rejected, knowing that it is you, not a function or a mask, that has been rejected.

Many persons avoid becoming even slightly vulnerable to others. Having been rejected before, they must protect themselves against such experiences. Thus they build their masks as protective devices. This insures that their experiences with others remain on the surface, on the level at which there is no risk of pain and suffering. Their masks multiply to meet the various situations which arise. The masks grow as they diversify, and exercise more and more autonomy in relationships.

Some persons in this way lose contact with their subject-selves. They assume so many roles with each other and with themselves that they lose the ability to retain that experiential insight into the distinction between their actions and their essence, their object-selves and their subject-selves. They are unable to establish a self-identity, an ability to act consistently from within. Or they choose not to exercise or implement that ability in their lives, thus granting to their masks an increasingly autonomous function.[6]

3. ALIENATION: THE NEED FOR REDEMPTION

When the object-self is separated from the subject-self, alienation results. The roles and masks intervene, become obstacles,

[6] Cf. A. Maslow, *Motivation and Personality* (New York: Harper & Brothers, 1954), ch. 13.

and gradually isolate the subject-self from the world of shared experience. There is a twofold alienation which occurs: incentric, when the person becomes alienated from his own center; and excentric, when the roles and masks gain autonomy sufficient to provide an impregnable barrier to personal unity with others, center-to-center.

In the last chapter we described the vision of Father Teilhard de Chardin. We noticed that, with the leap from life to mind, to noogenesis, there came into being, conscious and free megaparticles of matter. They could proceed toward divergence, becoming more individualistic and isolated; or toward convergence, safeguarding both the values of individual uniqueness and community, center-to-center unity with other persons. Roles and masks are the means by which conscious megaparticles isolate themselves, and pursue a goal of divergence instead of convergence.

Persons do not mature, or fail to do so, in a vacuum. We have discussed the necessity of considering the significant influences of environment on the development of human personality. There are some environments which are more conducive to convergent personal evolution than others. There are some environments which, in other words, naturally influence children in the process of maturation to act from within, to cultivate a natural trust of other people and openness to them.

There are other environments for which the opposite is true. Persons do not arbitrarily decide at a given moment in their lives to begin manufacturing masks and playing roles, to begin living a life of alienation, continually existing on the surface. It is clear that some environments are extremely effective in programming the personality-developments of children. In an environment, for example, in which the parents continuously play roles with each other and with their children in which fear, distrust and dishonesty are present, the children will naturally contrast proclivities to assimilate these values. Even before they reach maturity, and begin consciously to attempt to determine themselves from within, it may be too late. Environments, both in the home and in the society as such in which persons develop, do enhance the possibilities that alienation will occur.

Every society includes within its environment certain unspoken but effective values and goals. Racism, present in most societies in the Western hemisphere, is not hereditary. Studies confirm the rapid rate of transition from racial indifference to bigotry in children who gradually assimilate racist attitudes as they develop in their societies.

To summarize: there is an experientially intuited distinction between the subject-self and the object-self. These are not two different selves, but two selves which contribute to the total personality. The object-self is functionally necessary for establishing preliminary contacts with other persons, and for carrying on the normal activities demanded by life in a society.

This is the social "arena" of the masks and the roles, in which they are useful and necessary. But there is the danger that, for whatever reason, the masks usurp the autonomy they are not meant to exercise. Alienation results when the person loses the ability to act from within, placing himself unknowingly in a situation in which his masks and roles are obstacles to interior integration. This alienation is both incentric and excentric. That is, masks alienate persons from their own centers and from one another. Finally, the tendency toward this alienation can be present in home and social environment.

What, in the preceding analysis, is specifically Christian? We have been talking about human psychological experiences, shared by most persons. This realization is itself an illustration of the point we are making. Because faith is a claim about this world and the value of human life, it necessarily must be adequate to human experience. The Christian, in articulating to himself various aspects of his faith, must realize that he need not be "religious," as much as he must make sense of human experience.

He need not deal exclusively with the "mysteries" in attempting to integrate his faith with human life.

This is true specifically for the questions we asked at the beginning of this chapter, which concerned the claim of Christian faith that Jesus Christ, the Son of God, has redeemed mankind from sin. The meaning of this statement of faith can be indicated in the terms we have utilized so far in this chapter. Personal experience provides a basis for the Christian's claim that Christ is Redeemer.

With this basis and these concepts, we can now proceed to reflect on Christian teaching concerning "original sin," "redemption," and "grace." Is there a way to understand these "doctrines" which can be integrated with human experience, and will be intelligible in terminology arising from it?

4. ORIGINAL SIN

When the Christian expresses his belief in the "doctrine" of original sin, he need not experience, psychologically, the necessity to retreat from the world of normal human experience into the area of "religion." His belief concerning original sin involves a claim to recognize and experience alienation in human life as a universal condition. The brief analysis which follows is one way in which a Christian might articulate to himself his faith-understanding of the doctrine of original sin, without experiencing that yawning gap between the normal world and that of his religious beliefs.

When human life first appeared on this planet during the process of evolution, there came into being conscious and free megaparticles. They carried within them into the process the possibility for self-alienation, for divergent evolution, for self-conscious beings gradually to isolate themselves, instead of recognizing and implementing the basic and positive direction of the evolutionary process.

Biblical studies make it fairly clear that it is not necessary to believe that there was an historical individual, by the name of Adam, in order to understand the doctrine of original sin. There are many fine studies in this area, which analyze the correspondence between the Church's teaching and the mounting evidence in anthropology. Most of these works conclude in favor of the thesis that human life originated in small groups, rather than from a single male and female. Two excellent books are those of Father Robert North and Father Piet Schoonenberg, both of which demonstrate that a belief in the literal and historical existence of Adam and Eve is not demanded for an accurate reading of the Old Testament, much less for an understanding of the doctrine of original sin.[7]

What the doctrine does indicate is that early men exercised their ability to isolate themselves, to create masks and roles, and to make them autonomous. Whatever the nature of the first specific sinful actions which occurred, there entered human history, by means of those actions, tendencies toward divergent evolution, toward the granting by individuals of autonomy to their object-selves, toward isolation. The first such action is important only insofar as it signals the entry into the process of evolution of megaparticles' freely-chosen isolation from one another.

We are here pointing to our discussion during the first part of this chapter, concerning the subject-self and the object-self and the possibilities for incentric and excentric alienation. This possibility of alienation was actualized in the lives of early men, more of whom came to grant autonomy to their masks and roles instead of making use of them in the preliminary encounters among human beings which is their proper function.

Because free decisions and actions constitute environments for the development of future generations of men, the fact that some early persons isolated themselves through selfish actions, fear or

[7] Cf. Robert G. North, *Teilhard and the Creation of the Soul* (Milwaukee: Bruce, 1967), for the best treatment of these questions. Also cf. Piet Schoonenberg, *Man and Sin*, trans. J. Donceel (Notre Dame, Ind.: University of Notre Dame Press, 1965).

hesitancy, contributed to the formation of an environment which slowly began to reflect values of isolationism and alienation. This environment-formation has occurred in every culture. As the population grew, and tribes encountered one another in various kinds of relationships, hostility instead of loving communion became the constant trait of human societies everywhere. There has never existed a period in human history which has not included warfare and hostility. Human evolution traces a development in the forms and effectiveness of hostility. As these environments were formed in different cultures, children born into these cultures, prior to any free choices which they had the opportunity to make, were conditioned to adopt and ratify the isolationistic values of those environments in their lives.

The acceptance of the doctrine of original sin, therefore, includes the recognition, based on one's own human experience and observation of the world, that persons are alienated from themselves and from each other. In living out values of selfishness, they create environments which condition future human beings to adopt the same values.

Included is the belief, moreover, that this is not the way it has to be. Divergence remains one option of human beings, not their only possible course of evolution. Persons are born into environments which, prior to their ability to begin expressing freedom, condition them to adopt attitudes of fear and distrust toward others. Environments condition persons to adopt values of self-assertion-at-the-expense-of-others, thus strengthening incentric and excentric human alienation.

What else does "original sin" mean? It is necessary once again to reflect on the human experience of alienation, the lack of integration between subject-self and object-self, and among human selves. When in a person's life does he first recognize that he is in fact playing roles, wearing masks? When does he see for the first time that his masks and roles not only exist, but that they are obstacles to his personal growth? Does this recognition occur automatically, at a certain age, such as twelve or sixteen? Apparently not. Some younger children demonstrate an amazing ability to integrate, to act from their centers, to trust and to love; while many adults have lost that ability, have long since disintegrated, have alienated themselves from their centers and from others because of their masks and roles. This ability to self-integrate, to begin acting from within, can occur only when the object-self is distinguished and recognized as an obstacle to personal growth. This demands love.

Picture a room. It has four walls and a door. There is a child in the room, sitting on the floor, playing with his toys. The child does not know that there is a world beyond the four walls of the room. Or, although he may have been told, he does not want to leave the room. The door in the room is not an obstacle to him. It is only with the call of another from outside, which reveals to him that there is in fact an outside, awakening within him the desire to proceed outside, that the door becomes an obstacle to him. It is that call from the outside which makes possible his recognition of the door as an obstacle, and awakens his desire to overcome it.

How does this analogy pertain to the discussion? Human beings are "self-ish," some more so than others. This fact is recognized in both Eastern and Western cultures. As we have seen, the Buddha pointed to the universality of human pain and suffering, presupposing that men by the simple fact that they are men share in this condition. All men are *concerned* with themselves as individuals. Simply using the word "I" in a sentence is, for the Buddha, a sign of the presence of craving and egotism. The only solution to evil and suffering is the cessation of all desire and personal involvement in life.

Social environments condition human beings, from infancy through childhood, to develop masks and roles. Selfishness becomes destructive when it becomes egotism, when it becomes alienatory: a matter of self-at-the-expense-of-others. Some human beings discover the extent to which they are selfish and do not allow themselves to reach the point of disintegration and alienation. Self-consciousness, the safeguarding and deepening of individual uniqueness, is one value which must be preserved and protected for the sake of enriching the unity among persons.

In our brief analogy of the room, the door symbolizes that "self-ishness" or egotism. It is an obstacle long before it is recognized to be one. It is not an unsurmountable obstacle, but one which must be overcome in order for sharing to occur. Like the child in the room, a person must eventually come to recognize the existence of the door as an obstacle, experiencing a desire to pass through it into the world outside, the shared world of human experience. This understanding, which brings with it the power to overcome the obstacle by awakening the desire to do so, must come from without.

The Sufi mystics in the Islamic tradition express these observations in their poetry. An early Sufi martyr, al-Hallaj (d. 922), wrote: "Betwixt me and Thee there lingers an 'it is I' that torments me. Ah, of thy love, take away this 'I' from between us."

Reflecting on the experience of human growth, most persons remember the love of another person for them as first having awakened them to the existence of their fundamental egotism, creating within them the desire and the ability to begin overcoming it. Only love raises conscious megaparticles center-to-center, and draws upon the self-replenishing energy necessary to conquer egotism and isolationism, as we saw in terms of the analysis of Father Teilhard de Chardin.

Father Piet Fransen, S.J., in his book *Divine Grace and Man*, tells of a young woman who experiences herself to be loved for the first time.[8] She becomes more careful about her appearance —her clothes, her hair, her smile. She feels like a new person

[8] Cf. Peter Fransen, *Divine Grace and Man* (New York: Desclee, 1962), pp. 43–46.

and experiences a depth of living which she had not shared previously. She notices more young lovers, as her selective perception widens and deepens. She experiences a new kind of joy, as well as the possibilities for a new depth of pain and suffering, when she becomes vulnerable to another. She feels unworthy of the love of her young man, understanding experientially that his love for her is a gift, totally undeserved. Love is a reality which cannot be demanded. It can only be given and accepted freely, without guilt.

Most persons find, upon reflection, that their ability to recognize their masks and roles, as well as the desire to overcome them as obstacles, first appeared in their initial experience of being loved freely by another person. Recognizing the masks is essential for the development of a love relationship. Playing roles isolates lovers from each other. It is frustrating to hurt the person whom they love unnecessarily, as a result of wearing a certain mask or playing a certain role.

So often lovers cause the most pain for each other in ways which should not be. In thoughtless attempts to protect the loved one from possible future disappointment, the lover forces himself to act indifferently toward her. She, however, as a result of that kind of intuition operative in love relationships, instinctively pierces the masks and the roles, recognizes a lack of coherence and suffers unnecessarily. Masks and roles should not exist between lovers. If a love relationship is really to grow rich and fruitful, it has to pass beyond the stage of superficial comradeship. Love is a personal unity, center-to-center. Comradeship is often the union of masks and roles. Object-selves constitute comradeship; they can be obstacles to love.

These observations shed some light on human experience as such, and are basic to an understanding of the teaching concerning original sin. Why? If it is true that our present social environment includes values of selfishness, then it is possible to come to some conclusions concerning the past. For present environments are created by past decisions and actions.

Consider once again the family situation. If, in a given family, all the children are extremely possessive and acquisitive, consistently hesitant to share their toys with one another and other children, chances are that their parents embody in their lives those very values. Father may be a businessman, who continually discusses the methods he employs to amass profits in the "dog-eat-dog" world of capitalistic competition. Horatio Alger, the self-made man: this is his ideal. Violent conduct as a solution to problems of all kinds in our society is the logical extension of the extolling of the virtue of self-assertion.

If the parents in a family live according to these values, they do so at least partly because they, as members of a society, have also been conditioned. Present environmental values indicate the introduction of these values into the environment during the past.

Because of the entry and determinative influence of alienation in noogenetic evolution, mankind continued as generations succeeded generations to create and strengthen environments within the proclivity to love genuinely from within became increasingly difficult to recognize and implement. Like an individual person, mankind as such found itself in a condition of alienation, inside four walls, relatively oblivious to the door, the obstacle of egotism and disintegration.

Christians thus notice the presence of human alienation in the lives of men in their environments, prior to their making any free choices. They understand that mankind as such has need for the effective call addressed to it from outside itself. Mankind as such stands in need of redemption, of integration.

The Christian knows that human beings have been thinking, writing, speaking and praying about evil and salvation longer than they have been thinking and writing about any other topic. He may have read the philosophers, ancient and modern, and learned that an examination of human existence from within, in search of a meaning and value, comes to no definite conclusion if there is no awareness of transcendence in human life. As

John Macquarrie has shown, an analysis of human existence which takes no account of the possibility of men's interrelationship within a transcendent context, ends with the inability to reconcile basic tensions. If there is indeed meaning in human life, it must be recognized as the answer not completely supplied by the phenomenon of man.[9] Experiences of hope and frustration, moral purpose and failure, time and timelessness: these are examples of the tensions, the contrary experiences in human life, which do not resolve themselves. If they are intelligible, the analysis of their intelligibility must include an examination of the universal fact of death.

Human life, like the planet earth, becomes intelligible only when it is seen in context, in relationship.[10] The analysis of the process of evolution on the level of mind led Father Teilhard de Chardin to affirm the meaning and value of human life in itself, because the process revealed the presence and activity of Omega.

For the Christian to claim, therefore, that mankind stands in need of integration, humanization or redemption, is not to bring God in through a side door, as it were, or to try to maintain that it is God, not men, who is valuable. God or man—that is a choice which too many feel themselves forced to make. To understand that men need integration through love is not to become sentimental and cynical about the human condition, understanding men as intrinsically rotten and incurably evil. It is rather to claim that individual human beings and mankind as such are valuable in themselves when they are seen in their true context: for they are meant to be redeemed.

To affirm the necessity of redemption for mankind as such is to claim that such redemption must be, as it is for individual persons, revelatory and effective. Recognition and the ability to overcome: both are necessary. Redemption must be, can only be,

---

9 Cf. John Macquarrie, *Principles of Christian Theology* (New York: Scribner's, 1966), ch. 2.

10 Cf. Geddes MacGregor, *op. cit.*, p. 139.

love. Love alone reveals alienation and effects the overcoming
of it. The term which Christians utilize to name the love of
God, the loving Being-for-men of God, which simultaneously reveals to men their condition of alienation and effectively calls
for their progressive integration or redemption, is "grace."

5. "GOD WAS IN CHRIST, RECONCILING MEN . . ."

In the second chapter, during the discussion of the phrase "God
acts in history," we indicated that the Christian does not claim
a knowledge of God-as-he-exists-in-himself, or the Hindu Brahman. Rather, Christian faith is "Christ-ian": totally specified in
terms of Christ. Christ is the Revelatory Event of God, who retroactively reveals the significance and value of human life in this
world. Thus, accepting Christ in faith is making a claim to understand that significance and work to implement that value.

It is now possible to reflect further upon the meaning of the
Incarnation of Jesus Christ, so as to see how, in terms of our
analysis in this chapter, the Christian might articulate to himself the meaning of his belief in the divine redemption of men
by Christ.

The Incarnation is the event which makes sense of everything
for the Christian. It sheds light on the fact and depth of alienation in human life, as well as on the nature and power of the
redemptive presence which he recognizes to be operative in human history. As St. Paul indicated in his Epistle to the Romans,
it is only with the Incarnation, Crucifixion and Resurrection of
Christ that the full understanding of alienation's (original sin's),
presence within the human condition is possible.

The Incarnation of Christ specifies the meaning of the statement, "God loves his people." We have seen that redemption for
mankind must be revelatory and effective: it must be love. In
order to maintain, therefore, that God really loves men, is really
redeeming mankind, it is necessary to realize that love as such,

even divine love, must satisfy certain conditions. Love has a meaning, because of which it is possible to say: some actions, such as murder or rape, are unloving. Love, divine or human, must be genuine in order to be effective.

The statement "I love you" on the lips of a young man is not in itself the sign of the presence of genuine love. Not only could it be a deliberate lie, which is often the case; but too many persons, love, or try to love, for the wrong motives. A love which proceeds either from basic, unhealthy insecurity, or from a power-crazed need to possess, is not genuine love. Too many persons claim to be loving, while refusing to acknowledge their masks and roles as obstacles. Too many "love relationships" are not genuine, but are merely situations in which two selves remain objects to one another, sharing a union of object-selves, but not a unity of subject-selves.

"I love you" on the lips of the person who refuses or fears to make himself vulnerable is a lie. The pledge of love by the person who remains ever distant and detached rings hollow. Real love costs. It involves risk. It makes the lover vulnerable. This is not to say that lovers should continually analyze or test their love by the quantity of suffering it brings to them. But the lover who takes refuge behind his masks with his beloved does not live wisely, well, or at all.

This is why the Christian's belief or claim to understand that Jesus of Nazareth, the Christ, is God, is meaningful and necessary for his understanding of human life. The proclamation of love for men, issuing from a God who remained through it all distant and unconcerned, totally unaffected by the response to his offer, would not be a genuine profession of love. The "I love you" addressed to mankind by a God who remained totally invulnerable would be shallow and ineffectual. If Jesus Christ is not divine, is not God, then the Christian's claim to understand this world and human life and to recognize and accept the gracious Being-of-God-for-men in human history, is all a deception. Even more destructive than an innocent deception, it is a lie. The issue is not "merely" the divinity or nondivinity of Jesus Christ: the issue is the entire content and meaning of Christian faith in its claim to an accurate understanding of this world as meaningful and valuable in terms of persons.

There have been many gods to which men have prayed and offered sacrifices, and many ways in which they have argued to God's existence. Allah, Atman, Indra, Ishvara, Unmoved Mover, the "God of the philosophers": none of these gods is truly vulnerable in his relationships with men.

The Christian's faith allows him to understand his world and his participation in human life in the world. It makes sense on the basis of his own experience and the history of humanity on this planet, when he understands and affirms the necessity for redemption. He can understand that it is the Incarnation alone which fulfills the necessary requirements for genuine divine redemption and integration.

Because love as such, divine or human, centers on the beloved, the Christian must, in professing his faith, realize that the "purpose" of divine love or grace is not the creation of a community of human beings totally oblivious to the world and to other human beings, living with their heads in the clouds, concerned with "religious" matters. If the purpose of the love of any lover were simply his own gratification through the response of the beloved, there would be no love present. "God made me to know, love and serve Him in this world, and to be happy with Him in the next." Such a statement does not reflect the activity of genuine love. Rather, as St. John tells us in his first epistle, God "made" us to love one another.

Love centers a person on his beloved, not on himself. This is also true for the Christian's claim that God loves men. If God's love for men had as its only purpose their adoration of him, it would not be genuine love. An acknowledgment of the love of God for men includes an acceptance of the responsibility to the man-centered as well as God-centered, to involve himself concretely and effectively in the humanization of the world. "By this shall men know that you are my disciples, that you have love, one for another." Because faith is a claim to understand this world and human existence, specified by the acknowledgment that God has acted in and through Christ to redeem mankind, it should be impossible for a person to call himself "Christian" if he concerns himself only with "religious" affairs. The gracious Being-of-God-for-men, or grace, means that God is man-centered. Christians cannot be less than that. The Incarnation speaks this truth; Jesus Christ implements this truth in the world, as a member of the human community.

Christ himself spoke, not about "religion," but about this world, about the kind of world it is. He indicated that, because of the way this world is, the only effective way for men to relate to each other is through loving brotherhood. He spoke primarily of God's love for men and of the necessity for men to love one another, and incarnated both in himself.

He not only spoke; he acted. As we have seen, the actions of Christ are revelatory of the meaning of God's being for men in the world. The healings and curings; the multiplication of the loaves and fishes; the raising of Lazarus from the dead: the life, teachings and actions of God-in-Christ were man-centered, ordered to the redemption through love of human beings from their situation of alienation. The Crucifixion is an event, part of the process of redemption. The Crucifixion of Christ means that the process whereby God has made himself vulnerable in love to mankind is total. "No greater love than this hath any man."

At the same time, the Crucifixion reveals a fact about human existence more clearly than any other single event in history. It reveals an historical fact which has contributed to the social environment of mankind ever since—that God-in-Christ has truly loved men. He had made himself vulnerable, and has been rejected. "Some, preferring the darkness to the light. . . ."

It is the Crucifixion which conditions the Christian's evaluation of the optimistic claims of the secular humanist. The Christian, whose understanding concerning the depth of evil and alienation in human life is confirmed by his own present experience as well as by his observation of humanity, is bound by his understanding of the meaning of Christ's Crucifixion to reject superficial analyses of the presence of evil. His experience, his understanding of the world in which he lives, and his insight into the meaning of the Crucifixion allow him to recognize the superficiality of the claim that the existence of evil is simply a result of the lack of education, or the lack of progress in technological advancement. Evil is deeper in human life than that. Most persons know themselves to be capable of evil, sometimes for no apparent reason. Although they may know what they should do in a given situation, they find themselves acting egotistically. Educational advancement, they know, does not automatically abolish selfishness.

The Crucifixion of Christ, which reveals that men sometimes irrationally prefer the darkness to the light, is an event unintelligible except in relation to the revelatory events prior and subsequent to it. If the death of Christ was the end, then the possibilities for men of real valuation and love of human persons effectively revealed in Christ do not really exist. If the Crucifixion of Christ by itself were to form and condition the faith of Christians, there would be no basis for loving human persons as ultimately valuable in themselves.

If death was the obliteration of Christ, it is the annihilation of human persons. If so, nobody—not even God himself—has the right to demand the total commitment to the building of this earth, the kind of sacrifice necessary for the sake of both present and future generations, that he does in fact demand. Only if death is not the destruction of human persons, if the seventy years or so of a person's life do not exhaust his total existence, is there sufficient basis for loving him totally. Only then does human action and interaction assume a transcendent value they would not possess if human beings were, in the last analysis, nothing but highly complicated rats.

The claim that Jesus Christ is divine and incarnate in matter, life and noogenesis is essential and germane to the Christian's understanding of human existence in this world. The Crucifixion of Christ was a most profound revelatory event. But Resurrection followed. Both events contribute to the Christ-Event as such. Christian Revelation, and faith as the acceptance of that Revelation, affirms the primacy of life, not death.

The Resurrection necessarily follows and retroactively reveals the full significance of Incarnation and Crucifixion. It is the Resurrection of Christ which "contains" in germ the full content of the Christian's profession of faith. It marks the continued presence of the redemptive love or grace of God within the process of evolution, within the human community; and provides the basis for hopeful confidence that the kingdom of God will indeed become, through the stewardship of redeemed and redeeming humanity, a reality on this earth.

The implications of an understanding of the meaning of the Resurrection are literally infinite. Its significance is distorted drastically by those who would view it as some kind of "proof" for Christ's divinity, divorcing it in its significance from the entire process of evolution, the presence of alienation in human life and the need for redemption. Christ is risen: this fact provides the possibilities for Christian faith and provides the only context for the understanding which it claims. It is an event which, once partially understood, necessarily directs men into the world, not away from it, or beyond it. It provides a unique way of understanding the world and human existence and of valuing both for themselves. It provides for men the effective desire to participate in the continuing process of redemption.

Human love itself, wherever it is human love genuinely, is redemptive. For redemption demands the integration of subject-selves with object-selves. The Resurrection of Christ specifies the love of God for men, and provides the basis for the love of Christians for one another and for all men. To the extent that any human person experiences liberation from his situation of alienation, an experience which can occur only through love, he experiences grace and redemption. The Christian must condition himself, in order to live consistently with the view of life which he accepts in Christ and designates "faith," to recognize the presence of integrating forces in human life, whether or not they are active within institutional religious boundaries.

This requires the ability to integrate, in terms of his vision of faith, Christian joy with gratitude for technology's increasing contributions to the alleviation of poverty and disease throughout the world. As Fr. Bernard Cooke has said, the Christian must learn to rejoice whenever he sees human beings becoming able to live humanly. Such humanization may take the form of raising the average educational level in a country, or implementing medical facilities to enable more people to transcend the brute necessity of staying alive despite virus disease. Whatever contributes in any way to the possibilities for human integration is redemptive.

The Christian must learn to accept this not *despite* his faith, to rejoice besides being a Christian; but to rejoice *because* he is a Christian. Obviously, rejoicing does not suffice. Being a Christian demands more than reciting the Nicene Creed and meditating on its mysteries. It demands much more from persons than remote and sympathetic observations. Accepting Christian Revelation is accepting a responsibility to humanize the world by redeeming persons.

Teachers redeem when they liberate young persons from undue extrinsic determination because of ignorance. Becoming wise is a process which opens up possibilities of choice and evolution for men. The vocation of teaching, although it may not be formally "religious," is Christian if it contributes to the integration of persons. Policemen, senators, firemen, Peace Corps workers, housewives: these people should not see their "secular" life as separate from their "Christian" life. Accepting Christian faith is accepting the way of Christ: his way of looking at this world and human life, and his way of acting to redeem them both.

6. THE CHRISTIAN COMMUNITY

We discussed before the twofold nature of alienation, and pointed to the necessity of love as the only reality which safeguards and strengthens the value of both individual uniqueness and community. Christian redemption includes, therefore, not only the humanization of individuals through love, but the formation of, and participation in, a community whose principal function is the structuring of an integrating or redemptive environment within the wider, alienatory environments in every culture.

Traditionally the sacrament of baptism has been linked in meaning and function with original sin. Some grammar school children still learn that baptism "washes away" original sin from their souls. This metaphor is itself partly responsible for the fact that baptism remains one of the sacraments which many Christians cannot integrate with their lives. They cannot cease to wonder what difference it makes to pour water over the heads of screaming babies. What has it accomplished, practically, in their children's lives?

It is difficult to believe that a God who has demonstrated himself to be loving in his relationship with men would wantonly either torture or banish eternally from his presence an infant who, through no fault of his own, happened to die before the water was poured and the words pronounced. Many criminals, apostates and atheists were baptized while infants. The way in which the doctrine of original sin is often understood does not clarify the situation or solve the problems. It is a "religious" matter, uncritically accepted by many.

Original sin, however, is meaningful in a wider context and described in other language than "religious." All human beings born into this world are, as we discussed earlier, determined almost totally at first. Every event which has occurred since the beginning of the process of evolution has contributed to the formation of the environments into which human beings are born. The experiences and events of infancy and early childhood are also influential for a person's character development, his evolving self-consciousness.

"Original sin" refers to the first human act of selfish isolationism, which introduced into human history and environments that tendency toward egotism which was to be implemented to greater degrees in the lives of individuals born during succeeding generations. It refers also to the environmental situation into which human beings are born, which, prior to their ability to determine themselves from within, to act from their centers, forms them to adopt isolationist and individualistic values, to fear others instead of trusting them, to seek self-assertive vocations and professions.

"Jesus saves" means that the Incarnation, Crucifixion and Resurrection of Jesus Christ alone interpret the statement "God loves his people." These events are redemptive because they meet completely the need for redemption present in disintegrated human lives. The total Revelation, that which is fully redemptive and empowering, is present in the human consciousness of the risen Christ and specified through the members of his body—the Christian community and all men who genuinely love.

Baptism means all of this. Through baptism the Christian community accepts into its midst an infant human being, and pledges to provide the kind of environment which is redemptive and integrating, rather than alienating and isolating. Naturally, that organ of the community which accepts the greatest responsibility for this task of providing a redemptive environment of love, in order that the child might naturally assume values of trust and community, is the family. The parents of the child to be baptized should be the sponsors; it is they who accept the primary responsibility to provide a loving environment for their children.

Baptism is a process which begins with the pouring of the water, the symbolic profession of faith by the Christian community and by the parents. If baptism is to be effective, what is symbolized must develop as the child actualizes his human potential, growing in freedom and knowledge. Baptism rests in its meaning upon a frank acknowledgment by the community that persons are formed importantly by their environments; and consequently that the environments should be redemptive. They should include love, which provides for coming-to-freedom of human beings. Just as original sin is effective by means of determinants in the familial and social environments in which persons mature, so also is grace. Parents' love for their children is meant to be redemptive.

The "character" of the sacrament of baptism refers to the process which begins for most Christians in infancy, of being placed in an environment in which they come, slowly, to assimilate the vision of Christian faith: to look at the world and to understand themselves as human persons, in the way in which Jesus Christ sees them in the world. Character is therefore a societal reality: it presupposes the existence of the person in a determinative society, being formed by certain values, in the slow process of coming to the ability to form values from the inside, from the center. Parents who, in rejecting the way in which they were raised by their own parents, make a vow to refrain from determining their children religiously in any way, are being unrealistic. They will determine their children's values, even if they attempt to refrain from doing so. The real question is *how*.

"Baptism takes away original sin by giving grace." That statement is "religious." It is one way in which the Christian acknowledges the formative influence of past and present values and events upon his children; recognizes that too many values inherent "naturally" in human societies are alienating, not integrating. The Christian thus attempts to provide an integrating environment for his child, one in which the child can develop his personal potential most fully, can learn to love as he learns to live as a human being. Children should not grow to maturity, automatically accepting the principle that, for example, wars are necessary and justifiable. Nor is competitive self-interest necessarily the noblest economic system.

Original sin is not "something" that can be "taken away." Baptism is not meant to be something that happens once during a person's life, in a church, later to be forgotten. Grace is not a supernatural "something" that works wonders independently of the persons involved, any more than love is operative independently of lovers. For grace is love.

There can be no separation, intellectually or practically, between what is humanly necessary and fulfilling, and grace. Whatever integrates human beings, or provides for their ability to integrate themselves, to be able to act from their centers, is not "merely" human. Whatever makes it possible for object-selves to reflect, instead of protect and isolate, subject-selves, is pre-Christian or formally Christian.

Sufficient degrees of material complexity and inward intensity were prerequisites for the leap from cosmogenesis to biogenesis. Sufficient degrees of material complexity, biological complexity and intensity were necessary for the leap from biogenesis to noogenesis. So also, to be Christian is first of all, necessarily, to be materially, organically and psychically human. Christian faith cannot allow him who professes it to isolate his Christian values from his human ones. Faith coherently sublimates human understanding and love. His Christian principles are not separated "religiously" from his "secular" ones.

7. GRACE AND MATURITY

One implication of this is that genuine human psychological maturity is only possible for a person with faith. This is to say that only Christians can be mature. But Christian faith provides for—indeed, it demands—genuine psychological maturity. What are the criteria for maturity, in the way we are using the term?

A mature person is one who lives from his center, with the abiding awareness of the distinction between his subject-self and object-self. He does not succumb to the temptation to identify himself according to the masks and roles by which others may identify him—whether those masks and roles be aggrandizing or demeaning. He is, in a word, truly honest: consistently acting from within, accepting other people as they are, able to function with the knowledge that his impressions of them are impressions of their object-selves, not definitions of their personalities. He is what A. Maslow calls a "self-actualizing" person, able to offer and to accept love without contrivance.[11] For it is in allowing the object-self to exercise autonomy that the inability to love and to be loved arises.

The mature person is one who can exercise what John Keats once referred to, in a letter to his brother, as "negative capability": the ability to hold opposed ideas in one's mind, and still be able to function effectively. Minor obstacles and disappointments do not destroy his purposiveness.

Dr. Viktor Frankl, in *Man's Search for Meaning*, has made a similar point; as has Gordon Allport, another respected psychologist.[12] The mature person is able to recognize meaning and purpose in human life and his own; and is therefore able to exhibit that purposiveness of intent and activity which is so nec-

11 Cf. Maslow, *op. cit.*, ch. 13.

12 Cf. Viktor Frankl, *Man's Search for Meaning* (New York: Washington Square Press, 1965). Also cf. Gordon Allport, "Is the Concept of Self Necessary?" in Talafous, *op cit.*, pp. 134-53.

essary for psychological health. Negatively put, the person who is consistently unstable—who, like a leaf in the breeze, finds himself carried and directed by events—is not mature. The mature person maintains the ability to act consistently from within, from a general recognition of meaning and purpose in life, as well as the specific awareness of particular goals in his own life. He retains that integrity in the midst of conflicting forces and events. Minor setbacks or postponements do not signal the failure of his life-project as such. He is able to accept pain and suffering, and to grow through them instead of being disintegrated. His horizon is expansive enough to allow him to look beyond the present moment, and retain his ability to work creatively to contribute to forming a human environment.

This kind of maturity cannot develop in a person who believes and acts according to the belief that this world and human existence are meaningless and absurd. If such a judgment upon human existence in the world were accurate, there would be no reason for anyone to live as if there were meaning and value instead. Christian faith thus demands and makes possible genuine maturity because it is a claim to understand this world, and an affirmation of the meaning and value of human existence in it.

If Christian faith were centered completely on God, and tended to form human beings unable to accept totally the value of constructive involvement in this world of men, it would be a destructive historical force. There are immature persons whose "faith" reflects and strengthens that maturity, absolving them from moral responsibility and protecting them from the fear of death. But such "faith" is not Christian. Faith, if it creates in persons who have professed it since early childhood an ability to separate and maintain a separation between the "natural" and the "supernatural," is not genuine faith.

This is not to say that only Christians are mature. Obviously, that is not true. Nor is it to address non-Christians, and to label them psychologically immature. The Christian, when he reflects on the reasons for his positive evaluation of and commitment to human beings in this life, in this world, can understand that his basis, the claim he makes in faith, is one which allows for maturity or integration. His faith is not an abstract belief in a transcendent God which calls him to live for the next life, accumulating merits in this life from the good works which he performs. It is rather a claim to understand this world and its meaning and value in terms of persons; a claim which makes possible and demands a growth in personal psychological maturity. The Christian has the responsibility to make a difference in this world, to affect the lives of other persons positively and humanly; and this is the most serious responsibility possible. His faith not only allows, but demands, that he take the world seriously and contribute to its humanization. Without that faith there would not be sufficient reason for doing so.

The professions of faith, both verbal and symbolic, in sacramental "moments," in no way introduce a duality into the lives of Christians. For faith is a claim to understanding in this world, and provides, in terms of Christ, a specification for that understanding. Moreover, faith effectively reveals the presence and depth of evil in human life, makes possible and demands personal integration of self and of others. Faith, to express it metaphorically, sees through the same "eyes" that reason and "ordinary" human wisdom do. It looks upon the same world and the same persons—not a "religious" world.

Human love is redemptive. The environments of persons can reflect values which are redemptive and integrating as well. That is the most important function of the Christian community, the Church, as such. The kingdom of God is the kingdom of redeemed men. The Christian community is meant to exist, not separately from the world and the rest of men, but as the avant-garde of the human community. It is meant to witness to and provide the kind of environment in which human persons can become free. The fact that the term "Christian community" is not equivalent to the term "institutional Church" does not alter the point. More will be said about this later.

Sacraments are symbolic actions of this avant-garde community. Baptism and confirmation are symbolic moments in the effective process by which a person is born and grows into maturity in a humanizing environment. Matrimony is a sacrament because human love itself, as grace, finds its most meaningful model in the Christ-Event; and bringing a child up in love is not only a "human" task, but a Christian one. Parents redeem each other and their children through their love. The Eucharistic moments in the lives of Christians are symbolic expressions of that acceptance of faith (in the widest sense), and are meant to strengthen both that faith and the community. Penance and the sacrament of the anointing both arise from the fact that the life of faith is societal as well as individual: that, negatively, the community's effectiveness as avant-garde witness to the kingdom of redeemed men is restricted and lessened by the selfish actions of members of that community, as well as by the physical illnesses to which some of the members are susceptible. Both sacraments, consequently, are symbolic expressions by the community of the desire to strengthen the bonds of brotherhood. The sacrament of orders exists, in part, because the community has need of, and the right to, the constant opportunity of exploring and deepening their faith-understanding, and to the Eucharistic moments in which to express it.

Reflections on the meaning of faith in relation to sacraments can be enlightening. However, too many Christians preserve that gap between their "religious" actions and their "secular" deeds. The Mass, for example, does not make it perfectly clear to all Catholics in this country that to which they are committing themselves when they say, "I believe in Jesus Christ." This is not only because the liturgical renewal has not succeeded in involving Christians in the Eucharistic celebration as it was meant to do. It is evident that Christians do not seem to be living up to their identity as the avant-garde human community. But to say that they should be, and why, can be valuable. For the ideals professed in faith are too easily kept separate from life.

The verbal profession of Christian faith cannot remain verbal in its results. There are ways to define or describe the "virtue" of Christian faith so as to allow for, at least intellectually, the separation between the "natural" and the "supernatural" worlds, as we have seen. To describe Christian faith in a wider context, such as that present in these pages, hopefully makes that separation and disintegration impossible to maintain intellectually, and should produce appropriate psychologically practical consequences. The ways in which faith is often described allow for the separation theoretically and practically; our description does not.

8. CONCLUSION

This chapter began with a question. Does the Christian teaching about redemption, its necessity and its actuality, relate to human experience in this world, or is it a "religious" truth, with no relationship with reasonable experience, no obligation to demonstrate its relevance to the lives of contemporary men? We attempted to indicate a response to this question which took its origin in the reflective psychological experience of human beings.

In terms, primarily, of the distinction, intuited experientially, between the subject-self and the object-self, we saw how the Christian can indeed recognize in human experience in this world the need for redemption, in the same way that he recognizes in himself the necessity for love to integrate his life.

Perhaps it is the necessity for persons to become aware of the need for redemption which is the most important point of all. The language describing the topic of redemption in the past often included emotional connotations which were maudlin and individualistic. As such, that language itself was part of the problem. "Jesus saves" still brings to many hearers of that phrase today those same emotional connotations. They think that Christianity demands that they feel thoroughly evil and worthless, and abandon all constructive effort in their own behalf, throwing themselves on the mercy of a God who died some time ago, and who will come again. So the language is partly the problem. We have tried to talk in the language of "self," and to specify the meaning of terms like "original sin" and "redemption."

But this is not to say that the problem is merely linguistic. It is not. The difficulty is that, whatever the language, a great many persons today do not understand what it means to be redeemed; thus they do not experience the need for redemption. Without the experience of that need, Christianity must appear as totally irrelevant. That does not mean that Christians must necessarily "feel" guilty and sinful at all times. The Christian is a person who, after thoughtful analysis of his own experience, and his experience with others, acknowledges the redeeming presence of love as the only effective agent for the continuing progress of the process of evolution. Christ is important and necessary because he gives meaning to that process.

What prevents or restricts men's awareness of their need for redemption? One human quality does precisely that: pride, or self-assurance. Christ is the loving and effective divine and human answer to a question which exists in men and in the human community. But the answer makes little sense without the question. The question, as we have seen, is not a question about the existence of a supernatural God who exists apart from the world. It is, rather, a question about this world and the meaning and value of human life in it. Is the world meaningful? Do human persons have an intrinsic and transcendent value, which gives a profound significance to the relationships among them?

To those for whom that question does not exist, Christ is necessarily irrelevant. So is Christian faith—or any faith, for that matter. The "Horatio Alger" individual, the self-made man, who exhausts his efforts in the pursuit of economic power and prestige, and succeeds in isolating himself comfortably from the needs of the deprived: such an individual does not need Christ, does not need redemption. The question arises: How many Horatio Algers in this country today can consciously and without fear of hypocrisy call themselves "Christian"? "Faith and reason are of two different orders. . . ."

Some people, because of a fear as to what the answers to serious questions about their faith may be, simply do not allow such questions to become real for them. Television, bridge parties, baseball games: there are myriads of diversions by which object-selves hide the important question from subject-selves.

Christians need not bring the message of fire and brimstone to such individuals. For that is not the message which Christians bear. They bear the Gospel, what they call the "good news." Good news should make people happy. To those persons who live on the surface of life, who, either through fear or contentment, neglect to ask the important question, the Christian's message of the need for redemption and its presence will come when it is asked for. Christians must show others the question existing within them.

Christians must, if they find themselves living in a society whose values are dehumanizing, attempt to implement humanizing ones, demonstrating the superiority of such values both theoretically and practically, in experience. If an accurate understanding of the need for divine redemption is integrated with their experience, it can be integrated with the experience of any human being. I am not here speaking of the practice of "converting" people to Christianity, which I will discuss briefly in the following chapter.

Christian faith is the claim to an accurate understanding of this world, human existence, and the gracious Being of God, . . . which understanding calls for and makes possible the humanization of men and the worship of God the Father in a community witnessing to the presence of his kingdom on earth. Our explanation of the description of faith given in the second chapter is nearly complete. It is now clear that it includes the necessity for the Christian, in order to designate himself as such, to understand his own need for redemption (grace) as well as the need of the human community as such; and to involve himself positively, though not necessarily "religiously," in the formation of the human community into a brotherhood.

9. SUGGESTED READINGS

Adam, Karl. *The Christ of Faith*. Trans. Joyce Crick. New York: Mentor Omega, 1962.

Baillie, Donald M. *God Was in Christ*. New York: Scribner's, 1948.

Brown, Raymond. *Jesus God and Man*. Milwaukee: Bruce, 1967.

Cooke, Bernard J. *Christian Sacraments and Christian Personality*. New York: Holt, Rinehart and Winston, 1965.

DeRosa, Peter. *God Our Saviour*. Milwaukee: Bruce, 1967.

Schillebeeckx, Edward. *Christ: The Sacrament of the Encounter with God*. New York: Sheed & Ward, 1964.

Schoonenberg, Piet. *God's World in the Making*. Techny, Ill.: Divine Word Publications, 1967.

5:PROBLEMS
OF FAITH (II)

In the first chapter we raised a number of questions which indicated a basic dualism or separation, a disintegration, in the lives of many Christians, between the concerns of faith and those of normal human experience. We then attempted to describe and explain the concept of faith in a way more adequate than those in which it has been defined since the First Vatican Council. Our explanation of that description is nearly complete. Having attempted in the following chapters to indicate the possibilities for the integration of Christian faith with the world of science and that of human experience, it remains to return to some of those questions raised in the first chapter. Some of the problems are made possible by a misunderstanding of the nature and claims of Christian faith, as should be evident by now. The misunderstanding is present in the minds of both Christians and non-Christians. In order to concentrate on genuine problems, it is necessary to recognize the existence of bogus ones.

1. "I BELIEVE IN 'GOD'."

The first series of questions which we discussed dealt with the problem experienced by many Christians in relating their "God-apart-from-the-world" meaningfully to this world of human experience. What difference does a God who lives and moves in a different "order" make to this one? Can the Christian in the Peace Corps articulate the difference that his faith in Christ makes to his own life, and honestly desire to share that with his humanist friend? Why is it so necessary to believe in the "divinity" of Jesus Christ?

Those questions in those forms are made possible by certain presuppositions about the nature of Christian faith. The questions presuppose that faith is centered primarily and exclusively on God, apart from this world, and on Christ, whose primary characteristic, divinity, means that he shares this separateness and irrelevance of that kind of God. They also presuppose that faith operates in a completely different order and world from this one.

Faith which is genuinely Christian makes no claims concerning a transcendent God who exists totally in another realm, indifferent and inaccessible to men. The Incarnation anchors the faith-understanding of all Christians in the historical Event of Jesus of Nazareth, the Christ. A Christian claims to encounter and to know, not "God," but God-acting-in-and-through-Jesus Christ. This God, unlike the Brahman of Vedantic Hindus or the Allah of Muslims, is accessible. This God, Father, has made himself vulnerable to men; has loved human beings in the only genuine way possible: by becoming involved with them in the matter and life of their world.

The project of demonstrating the relevance of a God-apart-from-the-world to Christians—or to anyone, for that matter—is doomed to failure: no wonder Christians experience frustration in their attempts to do so. This world is demonstrating daily that such a God makes no difference to it. The Christian claims in faith, however, that he encounters the gracious Being of God for men, a God who has involved himself in matter and humanity so completely that the destinies of each are forever fused.

The Christian claims that Jesus Christ is divine. This specifies his belief in God and allows for the integration of that belief with his life. As we saw in the last chapter, if Christ is not divine, then the claims of Christian faith about this world and the value of human life are false as well. Christian faith as such centers on Christ, who is incarnate and involved in human history.

Not taking the Incarnation seriously is disastrous for the reflective Christian who attempts to integrate his faith with his life. An example of the failure to "take Christ seriously" is the approach to original sin and redemption which still informs some catechetical programs today. Such an approach begins by explaining original sin in such a way as to ignore completely the evidence favoring the theory of evolution. It thus enhances the probability that Christian children who mature psychologically will discover the same irreconcilability between their understanding of original sin and redemption and their acknowledgment of the evidence in favor of evolution, as that encountered by their parents.

This ahistorical approach to the doctrine of original sin begins with Adam, the first human being, who is a kind of superman. He has all of the "natural" human characteristics, *plus* some extra gifts, known as "preternatural" gifts, such as the freedom from concupiscence and from death. He also has another extra gift: sanctifying grace, a sharing in the life of God. With his sin, Adam falls. He loses all the extra gifts, and retains only his natural attributes, those of a nature which itself is thereafter "wounded." Because of this plight of Adam, and the fact that Adam has transmitted this wounded human nature to all his descendants, God decided to send a redeemer. Jesus Christ becomes a sort of divine afterthought, whose mission is to restore the "extras" which Adam lost through his fall.

Such an approach, a caricature of which is outlined above, obviously cannot be formally reconciled with the evidence in favor of evolution.[1] The evidence indicates that the process of evolution moved from lower to higher stages of being as it proceeded, as we saw in the third chapter. The probability that the first man, as the first conscious megaparticle on the level of noogenesis, was perfectly human, and that the rest of human history has been a kind of recovery process, is nonexistent. Further-

---

[1] Cf. North, *op. cit.*, pp. 120–56. Also cf. DeRosa, *op. cit.*, part 1.

more, if the coming of Christ really depended upon whether or not the first man arbitrarily chose to sin, then the implication is clear. Christ is not intrinsic in the world, essentially involved in it. He is a superfluous factor, dependent on the free choice of one man. Consequently, as human beings become more satisfied with their natural accomplishments and with the efficacy of natural programs of actions and social involvement, it becomes ever more difficult to see the relevance of Christ to the world.

An understanding of the analysis of Fr. Teilhard de Chardin prohibits the Christian from attempting to reconcile an otherworldly Christ with this world. There is no such Christ. The Incarnation meets the human need for redemption. Given the free choice by God to create by way of convergent evolution, the redemptive Incarnation of Christ-Omega is necessary, not superfluous. He has been present since the beginning, effectively creating the possibilities for humanization. Redemption was necessary from the beginning, for, as we saw, the birth of thought and freedom marks the entry into the process of evolution of tendencies toward divergence and isolation.[2]

It is necessary for conscious and free megaparticles to realize that love is the sole practical force capable of maintaining the direction of the process of evolution forward and upward. Christ-Omega comes not as a superfluous addition to the world and to human life, but as the Revelatory Event in that process. The Incarnation is not an event simply "added to" the process. It is an event which both presupposes and depends upon the process for its possibility. In turn, the redemptive Incarnation of Christ fulfills the process and reveals its significance retroactively. As thought coherently sublimates matter and life by enabling them

[2] Cf. North, op. cit., pp. 130–56. The question of the relative necessity for Christ's Incarnation has received serious theological attention for hundreds of years. In my opinion, the vision of Fr. Teilhard de Chardin provides the most coherent approach to the question, because it emphasizes the gratuity of the Christ-Event, while demonstrating the intrinsic interdependence of Christ and humanity.

to participate in higher degrees of unity, Christ is the coherent sublimation of cosmogenesis, biogenesis and noogenesis. The genesis of life presupposed and retroactively revealed the significance of evolution on the level of cosmogenesis. The existence of conscious megaparticles presupposed high degrees of material and organic complexity, as well as inward intensity. Mind elevates matter and life to the level of unity attained by a living and conscious human person. So also the Incarnation of Christ-Omega presupposed all that had gone on before, elevating all of reality.

For Christ's Incarnation to be possible and intelligible, there had to evolve sufficient degrees of material, biological, individual and social complexity. In the same way, the genesis of mind demanded the prior evolution of matter and life. And it is the Incarnation which, as we have been discussing at some length in previous chapters, provides for the Christian the scale of values by which he understands the meaning of the process as such.

The Christian's faith in God, then, is complete and inadequate if understood simply as a belief in the existence of a transcendent God. For to claim that Christ is divine is primarily to understand something about this world and the meaning of human life. It is also to claim a knowledge of God, not in himself, but insofar as has made himself vulnerable to men, involving himself in matter and in life.

Furthermore, it is the Incarnation of Christ which specifies the Christian's assessment of the depth of evil in human life, as well as which effectively reveals the only manner in which evil can be overcome. Dangerous are claims about the causes of evil and suffering in this life which are too superficial. By teaching that evil is simply a lack in technology or education, for example, some persons imply that the eradication of evil will occur automatically with scientific advances in technology and education. Despair and disintegration are the products of such a view.

Both technology and education have advanced at a fantastic

rate during the past fifty years, all over the world. Yet pain and suffering, and human alienation in all its forms, have not disappeared. On the contrary, to listen to many contemporary artists is to encounter the cries of pessimism and hopelessness.[3] The novels of Jean-Paul Sartre and Albert Camus, the plays of Archibald MacLeish and Arthur Miller, the "theatre of the absurd," abstract art—all reflect an age of both incredible human technological advances and human brokenness and despair. It is almost as if the artists and seers, who mirror in their work what they perceive in human life, are so deeply bitter precisely because the optimistic promises of a century ago have not come true. It would not be so poignantly disappointing had men not been promised by optimistic humanists that needless suffering would disappear completely with the advances in medicine. Instead wars, inflicting the most needless human sufferings imaginable, continue to wreak destruction and death. How will men ever eradicate them?

Christ's intrinsic relevance is apparent to the Christian, partly because it is the Incarnation, life, teachings and actions of Christ which reveal the depth and influence of evil in individual human persons and in human life as such. Only a vision of life which accounts for the depth of evil can be adequate in speaking to the possibilities for redemption from evil. Christ is necessary because he means that evil can be overcome through human integration and brotherhood, as we discussed in the fourth chapter.

We encounter here in slightly different form the traditional unity of the "theological virtues" of faith, hope, and love. Faith is the claim concerning the necessity for brotherly love, as we have seen. Hope is basically confidence. In hope, the Christian, in his realistic assessment of the past, recognizes the growth of the human community toward convergence—a growth which has occurred through pain. But no person is isolated. Hope arises

[3] Cf. William Barrett, *Irrational Man* (Garden City, N.Y.: Doubleday, 1958), chs. 1–2, for an enlightening discussion of the relationship between contemporary existentialist literature and the world it reflects.

out of the Christian's awareness that he is not alone, that his humanizing actions will contribute with those of his brothers to the effecting of the kingdom.

Without the Revelation of the love of God, human existence would indeed be ambiguous—and absurd in its ambiguity. This should be clear to the Christian, both from the perspective of the process of evolution and from a thoughtful analysis of his own being as subject-self and object-self.

To claim that Jesus is Lord, consequently, is to say something very important about this world and about human existence. The issue between the Christian and the humanist is not the abstract question of the existence of a totally transcendent God. It is the meaning and value of this world, human life, and the reasons for a commitment to human ideals and persons in an effort to make a difference in this world. The issue is a practical one.

If describing faith in terms of a belief in God and an afterlife has in the past contributed significantly to a fruitless series of debates between Christians and humanists, then an adequate description and understanding of Christian faith will begin to place the "conflict" in its proper context: in this world, concerned with the meaning of human life. The frustration resulting from the attempt to argue about the importance of a God apart from this world is an indication of the restricted value of the whole debate. That is not the issue. That is not the God of Christianity. The issue is the meaning of human life; and the God is the Father of Jesus Christ, whose Revelation concerns men in this world.

If the Christian feels that his moral principles and religious life rest completely on the existence of God, then his inability to constrain the assent of unbelievers will be psychologically destructive for him. It would be psychologically destructive for the painter to demonstrate that beauty exists, and that it can be recognized by human beings. It would be similarly destructive for the chemist to exhaust his energies in the attempt to prove that scientific experimentation is a valuable human activity. For Christians to become completely absorbed in an unnecessary and fruitless form of "proving" the first principles of their faith, is to waste their own time as well as that of others.

Fundamental Christian principles are in fact most reasonable. But the reasonable exploration of Christian faith, theology, takes place within the Christian community of faith, not outside it. The important task for Christians is not to engage in fruitless attempts to "prove" the existence of a supernatural being to unbelievers. It is rather for Christians themselves to understand why and how their faith makes the most sense of their world and their human experience. The enterprise of faith-integration occurs in this sphere of reality and in no other.

2. FAITH AND REASON

This observation brings us to the second series of questions discussed in the first chapter. These questions directly concern the reasonableness of faith, and proceed from the presupposition that faith and reason are, respectively, supernatural and natural activities. Thus, when reasonable persons seek to understand the "natural" world, "faith" has no function.

The language of faith, moreover, because it is centered exclusively on a being who by definition is totally inaccessible, is meaningless, because it cannot be verified through ordinary sense experience. These presuppositions are present in statements such as, "Reason can take one so far; then faith takes over." The impression forms that faith takes us to "never-never land," where all normal criteria for assessing the meaning of statements, and their truth or falsity, are completely abandoned.

It is important to emphasize strongly that the false conflicts and debates concerning faith and reason take their origin, to a great extent, in the way Christians themselves have described their understanding of faith. Catholics especially are educated from earliest childhood instinctively to separate faith and reason, in an attempt to safeguard the teaching that faith is a gift from God. It is possible, however, to affirm the gratuity of the Revelation of Christ and the vision of faith, without at the same time being forced to acknowledge a serious dichotomy between faith and reason. Faith is a gift. It is not a general understanding of human life. It is Christ's understanding, intelligible only in the realization that Christ is Redeemer. No Christian is the origin of his own faith-vision. Although faith and reason are noetic or knowing activities, they are not completely identical activities. Although reason never ceases to function in Christian faith, reason does not exhaust the realities of faith.

The Christian, in terms of his faith, lives in and makes claims about this world. His understanding of this world includes an insight into its intelligibility in terms of the Event of Christ. Christ does not reveal another world; he reveals the meaning and value of this one. He makes it clear that men must love one another, not simply because it is a nice thing to do; but because it is human love which is redemptive, which alone can provide for the progress of the process of evolution. Because this fundamental claim of the Christian in faith is centered in this world, evidence is admissible. It is necessary that the Christian discover in his study of the process of evolution or the structures of human personality factors which confirm the affirmation he makes in faith. His "religious" language, insofar as it is based on worldly processes and human experience, is meaningful.

This is not a "pat" solution to an extremely complicated metaphysical question, viz., the possibilities for the human intellect to apprehend the divine essence, and to articulate, at least negatively, an understanding of that essence.[4] But the whole problem is intensified unnecessarily for the Christian by presuppositions

---

[4] Cf. E. Mascall, op. cit., for an excellent discussion by a non-Catholic author of the Thomistic understanding of the analogy of being.

which make his faith out to be exclusively God-centered and otherworldly. To claim that the process of evolution finds its meaning and value in terms of persons is to speak meaningfully, and is to speak to an issue to which evidence can be offered as tending to verify or falsify that claim.

The contemporary "dialogue" between science and religion is extensive; some fine volumes in this area were recommended in the first chapter. Without indulging in excessive detail, it is necessary to specify somewhat the meaning of the terms "verify" and "falsify" within the scientific community. Our discussion of the extent to which the claims of Christian faith are capable of verification will then be more fruitful.

Discussions between scientific atheists and believers are often based upon inadequate presuppositions concerning the claims of scientific knowledge to truth. The kind of faith which some religious persons exhibited in days of old, which was a complete and blind belief in the power of God as a universal problem-solver, is inadequate. Accordingly, the kind of blind faith in science which characterizes the religious observations of some individuals in our own day is equally inadequate. For some people, science has replaced God: science knows all, science can do all, science will redeem mankind. Science has replaced God as a "stopgap" solution to problems not presently soluble.

It is important to remember, however, that persons whose comments concerning religion reflect that "stopgap" mentality are rarely members of the scientific community. Similarly, genuine scientists are careful to indicate the nature of the claims of scientific knowledge. It is an easy task to demonstrate the irreconcilability of science and religion only for the scientifically ignorant or the religiously immature.

Scientific knowledge is not a synonym for "certain knowledge." The scientific enterprise itself rests upon a kind of faith: a belief that the world and the universe operate according to laws capable of being recognized and utilized for the service of men. Now, this observation is not of crucial importance. But it is an indication that the simple equations, science = knowledge, faith = guesswork, are inaccurate. No longer do scientists claim absolute noetic certitude. Science is human knowledge.

The presupposition that the universe is ordered, is cosmos, and therefore accessible to scientific prediction on the basis of recurring patterns of natural phenomena, makes science possible. That particular presupposition cannot be verified conclusively; if it could, then the believer's argument for existence of God based on the observation of order in the universe would be rationally unassailable.[5]

The scientist examines the phenomenal world, that world capable of being measured and tested. Notice that the phrase is "capable of being measured and tested," not "capable of being observed or sensed." No one has ever seen an atom; yet high school students reproduce the periodic table of elements for their examinations, including the atomic numbers and weights of all the elements.[6] The claims of science to knowledge are restricted inherently only to those dimensions of the world which are susceptible to measurement and testing, as we have seen.

The world in which men live is a richer world than that. Albert Dondeyne, in making this point, uses the example of a shooting.[7] What happens scientifically when a man shoots another man? The physicist can measure the velocity of the bullet, its trajectory as affected by x gravitational force, the force of impact as it enters the body, et cetera. The chemist can analyze the gunpowder and test the gun barrel against the bullet to confirm that the bullet was fired from this particular gun. The biologist can examine the wound, and report on the extent of bleeding

5 Cf. Ian Barbour, *Issues in Science and Religion* (Englewood Cliffs, N.J.: Prentice-Hall, 1963), pp. 238–70. Also cf. Donald Walhout, ed., *Interpreting Religion* (Englewood Cliffs, N.J.: Prentice-Hall, 1963), pp. 113–46.

6 Cf. J. W. N. Sullivan, *The Limitations of Science* (New York: Viking Press, 1933), pp. 31–34.

7 A. Dondeyne, "The Existence of God in Contemporary Materialism," in C. Talafous, *op. cit.*, pp. 221–22.

and organic damage. The most important questions of all, concerning the meaning of the series of actions, go unanswered. Why was this man shot? Was the shooting a murderous action? Was it self-defense? Was it in time of war or peace? Questions of meaning and purpose are real questions, demanding satisfactory answers. Scientific investigation as such cannot be expected to supply these answers. If the only world acknowledged as real were this world insofar as it is accessible to scientific analysis, observation and measurement, we would, as Professor De Koninck has said, be living in a hollow world, devoid of meaning and purpose.

There are few philosophers today who would commit themselves to a defense of the verification principle in the form in which it was first proposed. This principle, significant in the discussion of religious language in the 1930's and 1940's, stipulated that, in order to be meaningful, a statement must be empirically verifiable, or mathematically or logically tautological. Strict adherence to that principle would disallow as meaningless statements of memory, purpose or value. That the rules for the meaningfulness of language have evolved, however, does not absolve the believer of the responsibility to speak clearly, in words anchored in concrete reality, not merely in other words.

It is true that language about a God defined as beyond sense experience in every way is relatively meaningless to a person who does not or cannot acknowledge the existence of such a being. What, then, about the language of Christian faith? With Thomas MacPherson we would note that Christian faith does not involve a claim to knowledge of God as he exists in himself.[8] Christian faith is "Christ-ian": totally specified in terms of Christ. Jesus of Nazareth, an historical individual, is the Christ. This means that the language of Christian faith concerning God is grounded in this world and in human experience.

8 Thomas MacPherson, *The Philosophy of Religion* (London: D. Van Nostrand, 1965), pp. 182–96.

It means also that to define faith in a wider context, as we have attempted to do, is to eliminate some of the problems. For two very important components of our description of faith are statements about the world and human existence in the world. If faith does include such claims, then its language must reflect it. Leaving aside for a moment the question of truth and falsity, the claims that the process of evolution manifests directionality, or that human persons stand in need of redemption, are meaningful. As we have seen, such claims can be verbalized in terms which draw upon biological evidence and human experience. Evidence is relevant to the discussion.

It is possible to assume a wider understanding of criteria for the meaningfulness of human discourse. But understanding the meaning of a statement necessarily implies neither its truth nor its falsity. The question of verifiability still remains. Philosophers of science have defined the term "verifiability" in a variety of ways. If a given statement is scientifically verifiable, it means that it is capable of being tested within a given scientific community, the members of which are pledged to as much objectivity as possible. In general, it means that evidence can be gathered, which tends either to confirm or distract from the claim of the statement.

It is especially important for our purposes to note that the processes of verification occur within a particular scientific community. For example, although Einstein's special theory of relativity may be verifiable or falsifiable, it is so only within the community of physicists. To persons with no background in physics, the process of verifying such a theory would be meaningless. One must understand the symbols in order to verify a theory within the scientific community.

A similar qualification must be made concerning the claims of faith. If evidence is indeed important to those claims, consideration of the evidence will be more fruitful for persons within the Christian community, whose background allows for a fuller participation in the community's symbolology. The Christian can recognize, both in the biology laboratory and in his own psychological experience, facts which tend to confirm his claim concerning the world. His claim, as a faith-claim, is a claim to knowledge and understanding. But just as no physicist would claim to be able to verify a scientific truth-claim to anybody and everybody, no Christian should believe himself capable of constraining the intellectual assent of unbelievers who do not choose to see the evidence he presents as absolutely conclusive.

3. "I BELIEVE IN THE RESURRECTION OF THE BODY."

As an illustration of these points, let us look briefly at one important Christian claim concerning human existence, that individual persons are of ultimate value because they are immortal. It is important to realize that, independently of the truth or falsity of the assertion, it provides a more reasonable and coherent basis for social involvement than its denial. It provides a better basis for loving persons and for sacrificing for the sake of a better humanity than does the claim that persons are not immortal. The actions of the Christian take on a dimension which would be absent if persons were nothing but super-rats. He must take persons seriously, not primarily because they were created by God in his image, but because persons themselves are not completely reducible to physical and temporal categories.

What are the possibilities for verifying such a claim for the Christian? What is there in human experience which tends to make the claim that persons are immortal a reasonable one? A "proof" designed to convince an atheist is not here the issue. Rather, much as it is possible to understand that "original sin" makes sense in terms of psychological experience, it should be possible to understand in similar terms the claim concerning personal immortality. It is to be expected, consequently, that in the experience of human persons there will be evidence. It will be of two kinds: that which tends to count against or falsify the assertion, and that which tends to confirm or to verify it.

We will consider some of the contrary experiences first. Sometimes our experiences incline us to feel much more mortal than immortal. When we are very sick, for example, it is obvious how bodily we creatures are. Serious illness, or an accident which includes a great deal of pain, can serve to impede the processes of "spirit" almost completely. Head injuries can alter personalities. Reflections on the process of growing old, senescence, bring home to us the contingency of our states of being.

Our experiences of the deaths of others leave very little hope in our minds for us, sometimes, of life beyond the grave. For death leaves persons so completely still. Except for doctors, nurses, morticians and others whose professions place them in constant contact with cadavers, most people find encounters with corpses to be unpleasant. The atmosphere which pervades so many funerals reflects this discomfort and apprehension. The ritualistic series of greetings, arrangements, holy cards, reverent silences, hearses—all of which obtain at funerals—is so often contrived.

Even the Christian community, which professes to believe that death is not the annihilation of a person, proceeds much of the time to act as if it were. The black vestments, the strange selections of scriptural passages, the arrangement of the bouquets and sprays behind the bier: the atmosphere, even in the churches, is so often contrived. It reflects in its contrivance that human uneasiness in the face of death.

It is true that since Vatican II, requiem services for the dead in some places have become more reflective of Christian faith, by including white vestments, Scriptural passages dealing with risen life, et cetera. But the morbid atmosphere is still extensively present. "May he rest in peace." This is to suggest that, if there is indeed everlasting life, it is a life of sleep, of unconsciousness and insensitivity. This type of perpetual rest does not present itself as an attractive goal to young people. For that matter, it leaves something to be desired for older people as well, who find much more satisfaction during their waking hours than they do while asleep.

Evelyn Waugh's *The Loved One* is a popular novel which satirizes some of the artificialities surrounding death in American society. Superficially the novel is amusing. But it is really not so funny to realize that the narrative descriptions in the novel are true to life.

Existentialist philosophers, although their books may not be read copiously by the majority of educated Americans, still have at least communicated one idea: that death and serious despair or anxiety are deeply related. People, whether they admit or not, are oftentimes deeply afraid of dying.

What can we conclude so far? Human beings, although they avoid the subject of death and the encounter with the phenomenon itself in others as much as possible, are extremely apprehensive concerning it. Some live in constant fear of death, others in such a way as to allow their object-selves to prevent the intrusion of the very topic into their thoughts and conversations. But the apprehensions and the fears are there, confirmed and strengthened in many cases not only by experience in the "secular" world of the "happy" mortuaries, but also in the churches.

It is necessary to be clear. I am not saying that our churches fail us when they conduct services which fail to manifest a happy certitude about the kind of immortal life which the deceased person is now leading. A certain apprehension concerning death seems to be normal and fairly universal, tending to make the claim that persons are immortal, based on human experience, rather tenuous.

It is common to contrast the accounts of the deaths of Jesus and of Socrates.[9] Socrates, who spent the last moments of his life in pleasant conversation with his colleagues, exhibited a calm

[9] Cf. Oscar Cullmann, "Immortality of the Soul or Resurrection of the Dead," in K. Stendahl, ed., *Immortality and Ressurection* (New York: Macmillan, 1965), pp. 17–18.

certitude about the immortality of his soul that we do not find in the Gospel accounts describing the hours preceding Christ's arrest and crucifixion. But it is a confidence born in the garden of olives, in the agony of the decision which he had to make.

Jesus' attitude toward death seems somehow more human than Socrates'. Persons, when they are honestly realistic, do experience apprehension as they assimilate into their consciousnesses the certain knowledge that they will die. The future, because it is unknown, sometimes gives rise to apprehension and fear. The apprehension of Jesus was not that his death would obliterate his being from existence. It included, at least in part, an uncertainty concerning the way in which he would continue to be. This attitude of Christ is meant to be assimilated by Christians. Claiming that persons are immortal is not to maintain that it is possible to prove the immortality of the soul to any reasonable person. It is a claim which, while it is open to the admission of evidence from human experience, is grounded ultimately in God the Father.

Most human beings experience apprehension in their reflections concerning their certain death. Such apprehensions grow out of their experiences or encounters with death, as well as their ignorance of the future. This is evidence which would tend to falsify the claim of Christian faith concerning personal immortality. The evidence, as we have seen, is present not only in the "secular" world, but in the "religious" sphere as well.

There are, however, elements in human experience and observation of the world which tend to provide confirmation for the claim that persons are immortal.

Common sense must apply here; this is not a "religious" claim which has no obligation to make sense. Perhaps the arguments and disputes concerning personal immortality, like those concerning the existence of God, have been made possible in large part by strange forms of Christian beliefs concerning death and immortality. For example, to explain that the resurrection of the body as a doctrine of faith means that, somehow, every human soul will be reunited with the very body present at the "prime of life" or at the moment of death, although the corpse has been sealed in the casket and buried in the ground, strains not only the powers of reason, but those of the imagination as well. Among the many problems which this form of belief causes is the fact that some persons apparently would find themselves, in the future, arguing or struggling over masses of molecules.

Consider the cannibal as an extreme example. Suppose he subdues an opponent in combat, a person in the prime of life. After preparing the body, the cannibal dines upon his erstwhile opponent. Matter which at one time "belonged" to his opponent is now part of the cannibal. The situation becomes more complicated still if, upon finishing his repast the cannibal himself is butchered and devoured by still another cannibal. Who, in some future life, is entitled to the matter now partially constituting the body of the third cannibal?

One wonders how reasonable persons could quietly and uncritically accept the above description of the doctrine of the resurrection of the body. Such a quiet acceptance is made possible by two presuppositions: (1) that teachings or doctrines of faith have no obligation to conform with common sense and reasonableness; and (2) that body, like soul, is a thing, a substance which comes into being at conception, remaining constant until death. Neither of these presuppositions is valid. Perhaps this form of belief in personal immortality, along with others equally incredulous, contributes to the macabre atmosphere surrounding deaths, funerals and burials to which we have been referring.

Such a belief also insults the rationality of unbelievers, and nourishes in them their appraisal of Christian faith as a fairytale. The way in which Christians articulate some propositional aspects of their faith has been partly responsible for the negative judgments by unbelievers concerning Christianity as a whole.

To repeat some key observations made earlier: the body is a process. It is the particular mass of matter informed at a given instant by person, spirit or within. The matter constituting my body is constantly changing. There is an intrinsic relationship between "me" and matter (the law of complexity-consciousness); but not between "me" and any particular matter in the universe. This is true for persons at the time of death. There is no necessary relationship between the matter constituting the corpse in the casket and the total person who has died. That body is not the person. Heaven will not include power struggles among persons over masses of molecules.

Persons do not exist in time and space except in a bodily manner. They are beings coherently sublimating matter: the within presupposes and elevates the without. Inward intensity demands a corresponding degree of outward complexity, as we have seen. Therefore, to think of death simply as the release of a spirit from its imprisonment in the body is to strain reasonableness. Continued personal life must be bodily, because men are evolutionary beings. But the term "body" must be understood, must be intelligible and adequate to experience.

Somewhat similar observations could be made concerning spirit or person. Although there is, as we discussed in the fourth chapter, an *I*, or reality which provides for the continuity-in-time of my experiences, still I constitute myself through decisions and actions. "I"—although the reality designated by that term cannot be defined, but only expressed—does not refer to a thing which somehow came into being intact at conception or birth and remains united with a body until death. Immutability is not a characteristic of human personality. Personal immortality, therefore, does not refer to a belief that death somehow freezes a person at an exact point in his evolution, completely cutting off his continued process of self-constitution. If so, it would not be personal immortality at all.

If it is necessary to reflect on our experiences to indicate what we do not mean by the claim that persons are immortal, it is possible to indicate on the same basis at least partially what we do mean, and to recognize confirmation in our experience of that claim.

A recollection of the discussion of the principle of retroactive revelation in the third chapter, in the system of Fr. Teilhard de Chardin, provides some valuable insights for present purposes. Through that principle we can recognize the genesis of conscious megaparticles of matter which, for the first time in the process of evolution, are able to recognize the significance of the process as such. The higher and later stages in the process provide vantage points from which to understand the direction of the process on the previous levels.

If it were possible to transport ourselves backward through time, to the moment just prior to the leap from cosmogenesis to biogenesis, retaining an understanding of the principle of retroactive revelation, we would find ourselves able to predict certain components of the beings which shortly would begin to exist.

For example, we would know that beings on the next level would manifest a high degree of material complexity. Without being able to forecast completely the arrival of life as such, we could at least be certain, from our understanding of cosmogenesis, that the next level would include and build upon the maximum degrees of material complexity and inward intensity present on the level of inorganic matter.

The same is true on the level of biogenesis. Without being able to predict the genesis of mind as such from the life-stage, we could describe many of the presuppositions necessary for the existence of mind: high degrees of material and organic complexity, stability, unity, et cetera. From what has gone before in the process, there emerges a stronger basis in present knowledge for predicting at least some of the necessary presuppositions for what will follow afterwards, if the process is true to its own principles.

Now let us return to the present. It is possible to predict certain prerequisite components of the process of human evolution. We have already discussed the convergent direction of the process, recognizing indications of the actual formation of a world community, whose members will become increasingly effective in their communications and lives of unity with one another.

What does this mean for our present purposes, in discussing the Christian claim to personal immortality? It necessarily conditions the way in which this claim must be expressed. For example, we know as evolutionary beings that future personal lives must involve both individual, personal consciousness, as well as an exceedingly intimate degree of unity among persons. We know, as evolutionary beings, that such existence must be bodily, with matter increasingly at the service of spirit. This must be true because of our present observation that matter is becoming increasingly at the service of spirit. We know that this future life will be personal, social, loving, and Christic—because Christ is revealed on the level of mind to be the meaning of the process. We know that it will be dynamic, not somnambulistic, because human persons constitute themselves in action, not in the cessation of all activity.

An interiorization of the principle of retroactive revelation should "demythologize" the form of the Christian's claim that persons are immortal. It should make impossible the unnecessarily logical and imaginary difficulties arising for those who attempt to describe their conception of future life in terms of the reuniting of particular bodies and souls.

It is necessary to direct attention inward, as well, to recognize elements in experience which provide the basis for the faith-claim that human persons are immortal. We have already noticed elements in our experience which seem to indicate the bondage of spirit to the processes of matter and time. Now let us notice experiences indicating the opposite influence as well.

Little children are sometimes amazed to discover certain powers which they possess. The fifth grader, for example, is so apprehensive concerning an imminent arithmetic examination that he wishes with all his might for an attack of a cold. He is pleasantly amazed to find himself on the morning of the scheduled examination actually coughing, sneezing and running a fever. Readers of Dr. Norman Vincent Peale's *The Power of Positive Thinking* find that they can program themselves to feel comfortable through concentration; but that they can produce uncomfortable physiological results as well.

Many persons, having taken instructions in autosuggestion or deep meditation, can slow down and stop their hearts, and can banish pain from a throbbing finger or thumb. All persons experience, besides the effect which "matter" has upon "spirit," for example in illness, the influence which "spirit" has on "matter." These experiences range from that of the adolescent at his first high school prom, whose apprehensive thoughts at the encounter with a certain young lady cause him to break out in a sweat, to the experiments of behavioral psychologists in bringing about the amazing results mentioned above, through hypnotic techniques. It is clear that many illnesses are, if not psychosomatic, at least psychosomatically related.

Senescence, or growing old, is unquestionably psychosomatic. Dr. Hinton, in his clinical study of dying persons' behavior referred to earlier, makes it clear that the elderly person becomes senile and dies because his desolation at becoming "useless" to so many people increases.[10] Conversely, some other people, involved in life actively beyond the age of retirement, exhibit no traces of senility prior to their deaths. "Growing old" is simply not solely a physiological process. Medical journals record the cases of older patients who remain alive against fantastic odds, surviving seemingly on their will to live alone.

This is not to indicate a "separation" within the human being. It indicates coherent sublimation: the mind does both presuppose and influence bodily functions. The mind does exhibit a determinative effect on the body, and operates according to

[10] Cf. John Hinton, *Dying* (Baltimore: Penguin Books, 1967), pp. 61–64.

principles which are not totally reducible to the laws of physics.

This becomes clearer in those experiences in which time, often considered a plodding, constantly identical passage from moment to moment, is experienced as relative. In such experiences the mind often performs at an operational velocity which leaves time behind. Many persons, for example, who have nearly died, remark that when they were actually confronted with their own dying, "their whole life flashed before their eyes." Others, perhaps after a fall or some other experience which measured perhaps one second, are amazed upon later reflection at the quantity of mental activity which occurred during that instant. The number of thoughts of which the mind is capable in an instant is astounding. The processes of mind sometimes exhibit a striking independence, although it is relative, from the laws of physics. For the mind operates according to its own laws.

Time is not a plodding thing. When a person is completely absorbed in a project, or totally attentive to another person, the velocity of time increases significantly. Time plods along most slowly in experiences of isolation, suffering: when the person becomes absorbed in introspection and isolation.

This discussion could proceed almost interminably. Memory, experiences of responsible self-examination: there are indications in our present observation of the world and our psychological experiences that persons are not totally accounted for in terms of the laws of physics. Nor are they completely accounted for by behavioral psychologists, whose observation of selves is, by definition, observation of object-selves. Experiences, even the same experiences, are not exactly the same for the experiencer and the observer.

4. BLIND FAITH? CHRISTIANS AND HUMANISTS

The preceding brief series of observations and reflections was an example of one manner in which to understand how "evidence" is relevant to the Christian's claim that persons do not cease to exist at the moment of death. The claim is a meaningful one, one which can be elaborated in terms arising from human experience and from an understanding of the process of evolution. It is also one which admits evidence to the discussion. It is a claim of faith which need not, and cannot, abandon the claim to reasonableness.

"Blind faith" is destructive in the lives of human beings. Christian faith is not blind. It is a meaningful claim to understanding, which allows for and demands the integration of that claim with life in this world, and with human experience.

It is necessary to make some observations concerning the "debate" between the Christian and the humanist to which we have referred from time to time throughout this book. Scientific knowledge, as scientific, presents no obstacle to Christian faith. It is simply invalid for anyone understanding the nature and claims of scientific knowledge to conclude that there is a death-struggle between science and faith. The "struggle," if you will, is between two faith-claims: that this world and human life are meaningful, and that human persons have a value in themselves because they do not cease to exist; and that the world is meaningless and absurd, that the lives of human persons are completely reducible to the laws of physics and chemistry, ceasing to exist at death. The conflict is not between science and religion; it is between atheism or agnosticism and Christian faith. Both are faith-claims about this world and human life. Evidence is therefore relevant to the discussion. Evidence is relevant for the Christian who, in the profession of his faith, recognizes elements in the world and in human experience which tend to confirm that faith-claim.

Faith in no way implies "living for God and for another world." It rather provides a basis for living in and for this world and for other persons, and is more adequate for personal and social involvement than the belief that life is meaningless.

Christian faith takes better account of human existence and

the world than the faith of the atheist, or the decision by the secular humanist to prescind from any claims (because of the belief that there are no answers to be found). It can, for example, take account of the directionality of the evolutionary process; experiences of moral responsibility, of love, and experiences indicating a relative independence of mind from matter. It provides a clear understanding of the necessity to love other men for themselves because they are intrinsically valuable. Christians' faith commits them to work creatively, in hope, to establish the components of the world communty in the process of being born.

There is indeed a serious issue for Christian faith. But to argue for the importance of a God-apart-from-the-world to a world which is the locus of all experience is to expend useless energy. The issue exists regarding important decisions which will affect the lives of all human beings in the future. The Christian must be able, because of his faith, not despite it, to work with men of every nation and religious persuasion, to implement principles to underly those important decisions, principles which safeguard human dignity and promote the convergence of mankind.

5. CONVERSIONS: THE QUESTION

The third series of questions in the first chapter concerned persons of other faiths. The question seems to be that of conversion: To what extent does the Christian's understanding of his faith impel him to "save" other men from ignorance and from damnation? We saw that a narrow conception of faith led nineteenth century Catholics logically to undertake a mandate to convert non-Christians, designated as ignorant in their superstitious practices and beliefs.

"Why be a Christian?" is a question which has two aspects: a within and a without. The Christian must be able to understand why his own faith remains so valuable. Are there any criteria, outside "religion" as such, which bear upon the assessment of the claims of different faiths upon men?

If the Christian, reflecting on criteria such as reasonableness, adequacy to human experience, coherence, consistency, et cetera, can articulate to his own satisfaction sufficient basis for his profession of faith, what should be his attitude toward those individuals who are outside the boundaries of institutional Christian forms?

We have described Christian faith as a claim to understand this world, and to recognize its meaning and value in terms of persons. We have also briefly discussed some of the ways in which this claim can be integrated with living in this world, experiencing as a person. This allows for two preliminary observations: (a) Every religious person must in some way account for this world and for the meaning of human existence, including the phenomenon of human personality and the event of death. This is a kind of criterion for the Christian, in reflecting upon the relationship of his own faith to those of other men: to what extent does this person account for such important phenomena? How do his accounts concur with experience and unbiased observation of the world? (b) To the degree that there is present in the faith of another an understanding of this world and the value of human life which is adequate, Christians are united with him in faith, not separated. Christ reveals a vision of reality, not a "religion."

Attempting to articulate aspects of the relationship between Christianity and other "religions" is a task which is much more fruitful when the starting point is not religion, but faith, in the way we have described it. Then one is primarily interested in what unites persons, and in the ways they understand their world and themselves—not in what separates them. The Christian can rejoice to find in the faiths of other men common respect for, and commitment to, human persons. He can recognize, wherever he sees the processes of humanization being implemented, the presence of grace. He can see that it really does make a difference whether or not human *persons* exist, or whether "person" simply denotes an imaginary, fictitious specter.

The Christian has to realize that the vision of life which he professes in faith, which he integrates practically as determining the way he lives, stands in judgment of religious institutions as such—including the particular institution to which he belongs. He cannot abide, for example, by the claim of a religious individual that women share the status of animals. But the reason he cannot accept that particular teaching is not just that it is not permitted by his Christian faith. It is because the claim is untrue. He has the right to expect from one who would attempt to constrain his intellectual agreement justification on the basis of what can be shown to be reasonable and true. He demands this much of his own faith; and he must bring similar criteria to bear in his examination of the faiths of other men.

This does not mean that one should expect from Christians overriding statements of evaluation, such as "Hinduism is untrue; Christianity is true." Unless he actually participates in the community of faith in which Hindus participate, he cannot possibly have the kind of understanding of that faith that Hindus themselves have. Similarly, he would deny that the rendition of his own Christian faith by a Hindu or a humanist actually conforms with what he understands by his profession of faith.[11]

Insofar as men as such, independently of their institutional membership, accept and live by humanizing values, the Christian shares their vision. No religion, by definition, can claim for itself as an institution to embody "the truth." The Christian's faith is in Christ as the way and the truth; and it is Christ's vision which he attempts to profess and to integrate into his own life.

What, then, are the demands of the new apologetic as regards the value of conversions? The old apologetic, as we know, was

11 Cf. Wilfred Cantwell Smith. *The Meaning and End of Religion* (New York: New American Library, 1964), pp. 174–81.

extremely interested in hastening the day when all men would be designated "Roman Catholic," either by accepting the gift of faith directly from God, or by being constrained rationally by God's agents in the Church to believe in him and in the divine mission of the Church. But if faith is a claim to understand, then it is not "something" which can be given to or forced upon anyone. In reflecting on the worldwide project of conversion, and attempting to assess its relative value, it is well to recall the manner in which conversions to the vision of Christ usually occur.

In our own society, "converts" arise for many reasons. Most often, however, the reason can be specified, in terms of an individual or a group of individuals. Usually it is in getting to know a Christian well that a non-Christian encounters Christian faith. For faith "exists" in persons. It is not a thing. Christians should be living according to the faith which they profess. If they were really doing so, others would ask what makes it possible for them to live in the way they do. Because their faith would be important to Christians, the answer would be: "Christ, and all that he entails."

In other words, Christ, and the vision of faith, must come as the answer to a question, one which emerges from within persons. It is needless, disrespectful of persons and clearly contrary to the principle of Christian faith to think of other persons as less than dignified because they do not happen to carry the Christian label.

It is true that Christ is important to Christians, that they should very much want to speak of him, and to share his vision with others. But others have to desire that first. They should encounter his vision in Christians. The point, expressed simply, is this: if Christians really lived according to their faith, troubling considerations concerning the conversions of unbelievers would not exist. It is not because of Christ that Christian membership is decreasing.

Converting begins at home, within the Christian community. Christians themselves have to understand what they are saying when they say, "I accept Jesus Christ." Involvement in liturgical renewal, in Christian educational programs for youth and for adults, realistic homilies by preachers which manifest authentic concern for social issues as well as a refusal to compromise for the sake of offending the wealthy members of the parish—all of these activities are missionary. Only with the faith-integration of Christians themselves will the possibilities for sharing Christ with others improve.

Doctors, artists, statesmen, teachers, social workers and volunteers—every Christian whose profession contributes to the implementing of the human community is Christianizing the world. Christians should have faith in Christ and believe that, when the sufficient degrees of humanization are present in the world, the conscious recognition of the Lordship of Christ by all men will come. The age of converting people to Christian institutional, it may be hoped, is gone; it was the product of a mentality within which Catholics narrowly understood the meaning of faith and were apparently extremely insecure in that faith.

6. INSTITUTIONAL CHRISTIAN FORMS

The last series of questions in the first chapter concerned the institutional forms of Christianity, specifically Roman Catholicism. Institutions modify the claims of the community to truth. This is to make a similar point to that of Charles Davis in his book, *A Question of Conscience,* that the cumbersome structures and slow processes of renewal, as well as the lack of honesty and personal respect in relationships between bishops and the faithful, taint and weaken the claim of the Catholic Church to be the avant-garde of the human community, the locus of the redemptive presence of Christ.[12]

12 Cf. Charles Davis, *A Question of Conscience* (New York: Harper & Row, 1967), pp. 45-61.

Why should a Catholic remain a Catholic instead of becoming a Methodist? This is another question concerning the institutional forms of Christianity. It can, therefore, be asked within the various Christian churches.

The first point to be made is that, of all the questions, this one does indeed come last. It arises last, not only chronologically, in this book, but in the Christian priority-scale of importance. The faith of each Christian provides the criteria by which he must assess the demands of each institutional form of Christianity upon him. That faith, in fact, judges every institution, and is fully or purely present in no single one of them.

Christ did not make membership in the Roman Catholic Church an integral element in his vision of life. Nor did he so construe membership in the Methodist, Presbyterian or Anglican churches. Ecumenists today are attempting to demolish the dishearteningly unnecessary barriers separating Christians from one another. They are doing so both on the level of doctrine, in ecumenical institutes and colloquia, and in the area of worship, in communal liturgical situations.

We have seen that Christian faith does demand membership in a community of faith. It is also true that the term "community of faith" is not absolutely synonymous with any particular Christian institutional form. The Catholic, then, works from his understanding of the meaning of faith to assess his membership in the Church. He understands the necessity for the existence and operation of a teaching authority within the community of faith, so that the propositional articulations of Christian faith are not allowed to obfuscate the experience of faith. There must be a contemporary norm, in terms of which the judgment as to the fidelity of specific interpretations of Christian faith can be made in every age.[13]

He can indeed recognize the existence and operation of such a teaching authority within the Catholic Church, reflecting con-

13 Cf. Chapter Two.

tinuity with past generations of Christians. The Catholic knows that, despite the apparent loss of papal prestige during the past two years or so, the Holy Father and his office possess considerable influence for the forces of humanization in the world. The world remembers the fairly recent appearance of the Holy Father before the United Nations, during which he spoke the words, "War never again."

The Catholic can accept the fact that the members of the magisterium are human and make mistakes, even when speaking concerning serious social issues. The encyclicals of the nineteenth century and the Syllabus of Errors, which condemned the teaching that all men have an inviolable right to worship according to the dictates of conscience, have been superseded by the documents of the Second Vatican Council, which manifest an evolution in that teaching.

The renewal presently occurring in the structures and functions of the magisterium will continue to take place. The form of the Catholic Church one hundred years from now will therefore be quite different from the form of the Church as it now exists. Being realistic about it, therefore, the Catholic can indeed see the value of calling himself a Catholic Christian.

Furthermore, his understanding of the Eucharist in the light of his faith allows him to recognize within the Catholic Church authentic expressions of that Eucharist. He knows that, for example, a Eucharistic celebration which is simply "in the memory of the late Jesus Christ" does not sufficiently account for the necessity and meaning of the Resurrection. It is crucial that Christ be really present to Christians in the context of that action. It is important to associate oneself with Christians whose propositional articulation of Christian faith expresses that truth. Such a community is the Catholic Church.

The Catholic Christian also understands, as he begins to integrate his faith practically with his life, the value and the necessity for worship of God the Father, in and through Christ, in the power of the Spirit. He knows that it is the love of God the Father, incarnate in Christ and made effective by the powerful presence of the Spirit in the world, which gives meaning to the world and to human existence, which allows him to understand that world and that existence, and take both of them seriously. The mature Catholic Christian is a celebrator. This is not to say that he is a perpetual "happy warrior," longing to be delivered from these earthly fetters. He is a realistic person who experiences grace, and who desires to express his gratitude, his Eucharist, and to continue to accept the responsibilities accruing to the title "Christian." He sees, in other words, the necessity and value of effective worship within the community of faith, to enable him to encounter Christ and his Father and to express his thanksgiving.

He encounters these values in the Catholic Church. Liturgical forms should both express and create the liturgical reality which they signify—the avant-garde Christian community. The forms, consequently, must be flexible enough to allow for uncontrived expressions of worship. There has for many years within the Catholic Church been a resistance to liturgical reform and elasticity. However, the situation is certainly better today because of the influence of a revitalized Catholic theological effort, as well as the openness of many bishops toward liturgical experimentation. There is reason to expect this slow process of liturgical renewal to continue. Catholics unable to implement needed reforms in their own parishes have a variety of options open to them, from economic boycott to participating in the life of another parish. Some of the bishops in this country have shown their willingness and eagerness to implement the liturgical reforms urged in the documents of Vatican II. They will continue to do so.

Many Catholics are scandalized by the wealth of their Church. The ownership of lands, corporations, stocks and bonds, including assets whose exact total does not seem to be available for public scrutiny, scandalizes because a Christian church should not have such vested interest in mammon. At the same time, without attempting to defend the accumulation of wealth in principle by the Church, the wealth of the Catholic Church does in fact benefit poor people all over the world. In this country alone there are thousands of Catholic social service institutions, such as orphanages, hospitals and homes for the aged, which are supported by the Church. The Catholic Bishops' Relief Fund has long been beneficial to persons in poverty areas throughout the world, recently receiving publicity because of its effectiveness in arranging aid for the citizens of Biafra.

That the Catholic Church is extremely wealthy means that the Church *can* do much more than it is already doing to establish and strengthen the forces of humanization. As Catholics begin to live out the vision professed in their faith, their institutions will reflect more accurately the values underlying that faith.

Among constructive suggestions in this area recently is that of Cardinal Suenens, who suggests that contemplative orders within the Church open the doors of their institutions to laymen and women, providing the opportunity for these people to make contact with the spiritual resources of the religious orders. The institutions will thus become more effective in the task of humanizing the world.[14]

The question of the relative importance of institutional Christian forms is important today. It is discussed in many contexts; optimists and pessimists abound. Without becoming more involved in this discussion, because it is not central to the thesis of this book, we can conclude that it is possible for the Catholic Christian to integrate his understanding of Christian faith with his membership in the Catholic community; as it is possible for the Methodist Christian to integrate his faith and his community. The Catholic recognizes the explicit presence of the essential elements of his vision of faith in his Church, as well as the con-

14 Cf. Suenens, *op. cit.*, ch. 4.

tinuous necessity for the institutional forms of that Church to maintain their processes of evolution. When the forms begin to enslave and dehumanize persons, they must change to serve persons. This is not to suggest that Catholics must make membership in the Catholic Church their paramount concern; such a concern is a luxury which they cannot now afford.

7. CONCLUSION

In concluding this rather cursory treatment of Christian faith and some of its implications, I once again offer the description of faith first articulated in chapter two. Christian faith is a claim to an accurate understanding of this world, human existence, and the gracious Being of God; and understanding which is given in the being, life, actions and teachings of Jesus Christ; and one which calls for and makes possible the humanization of men and the worship of God the Father in a community witnessing to the presence of his kingdom on earth.

It should now be clear that each phrase is important to an understanding of faith. It should also be clear that the description, as well as the discussion of its implications, is offered primarily for the reflections of Christians. These discussions have not been intended as "proofs" of anything. They have indicated how a narrow and inadequate conception of Christian faith can lead and has led, historically, to the formation of several questions and problems which should not exist. They have also attempted to point to some reasons for the necessity to expand our description of faith, along with the possibilities for integrating that expanded understanding with human life.

This book rests upon a presupposition which is perhaps suspect today in some theological circles. I speak of my conviction that it is important to think and talk about Christian doctrines and beliefs, and to explore their reasonableness. Some, forcing a choice, maintain that actions are more important. The choice must not be allowed to become disjunctive, an either-or. To ignore the need for rational scrutiny of faith by Christians is disastrous.

A narrow understanding of the nature and role of faith has in the past at least contributed to false questions in our own day, which have arisen in the practical order to cause degrees of disintegration in the minds of many Christians. An expanded concept of faith, its nature and function, will serve to counterbalance that practical influence. No Christian can claim absolute certitude that his profession of faith is completely accurate and objective. Doubt is an element in every human claim to truth. All Christians live according to their understanding of the meaning of Christian faith. As that meaning becomes clearer and more relevant, our lives as Christians should reflect more accurately and effectively the values which we profess.

INDEX